1000 RINGS

ACKNOWLEDGMENTS

The wisdom, enthusiasm, and dedication of Robert W. Ebendorf enabled me to create this book. He generously opened studio doors for me around the world and brought forth many of the great artists whose rings grace these pages. His consideration as a juror and author was equally dynamic. I am forever thankful and inspired.

I am also indebted to a first-class team of editorial assistants. Rebecca Lim, Nathalie Mornu, and Anne Hollyfield-Hesford undertook this project with fearless enthusiasm. Their tireless efforts and incredible attention to detail appear on every page. Special thanks to Rebecca for trusting me to steer us safely through the storm.

Thanks to the jewelers who contributed images for this publication. I feel very fortunate to have the opportunity to document part of your creative life.

Thank you to the many galleries that passionately support and promote contemporary jewelry. Special thanks to Veronika Schwarzinger of Galerie V & V, Vienna, Austria; Judy Donald of OXOXO Gallery, London, England; and Libby Cooper and JoAnne Cooper of Mobilia Gallery, Cambridge, Massachusetts for their assistance.

I am grateful to Dana Irwin and Lance Wille for skillfully designing these pages with taste and reverence.

Thanks to the loyal brain trust of Terry Taylor, Joanna Gollberg, Paige Gilchrist, and Rick Morris. You are my ignition pedal and my steering wheel.

Marthe Le Van

Experimentation keeps an artist alive and humble.
Yuki Murata

1000 RINGS

Inspiring Adornments for the Hand

Introduction by Robert W. Ebendorf

LARK BOOKS

A Division of Sterling Publishing Co., Inc.
New York

Editor: Marthe Le Van

Art Director: Dana Irwin

Cover Designer: Barbara Zaretsky

Assistant Editor: Rebecca Lim,
Nathalie Mornu,
Anne Hollyfield-Hesford

Assistant Art Director: Lance Wille

Editorial Assistance: Delores Gosnell,
Rosemary Kast

Editorial Intern: Rose McLarney,
Ryan Sniatecki, Meghan McGuire,
Amanda Wheeler

Proofreader: Misty M. Lees

Cover:
PATTY L. COKUS
Articulated Frusta: Ring #1, 2001
Photo by Douglas Yaple

Spine:
MARK NUELL
Untitled, 2003
Photo by Peter White

Back Cover, Top:
DEBORAH LOZIER
Untitled, 2001
Photo by Hap Sakwa

Back Cover, Bottom Left:
JACK and ELIZABETH GUALTIERI
Zaffiro Goldsmithing
Lotus Ring, 2001
Photo by Daniel Van Rossen

Back Cover, Bottom Right:
E. ELIZABETH PETERS
*Wrap Ring with Freshwater Baroque
Pearl and Aquamarine, 2002*
Photo by Petr Weigl

Front Flap:
ISABELLE POSILLICO
Hug, Kiss with a Spark, 2002
Photo by Hap Sakwa

Back Flap:
THOMAS MANN
Stone Fetish Rings, 2003
Photo by Angele Seiley

Title Page:
ADDAM
Fliight, 2002
Photo by Alan Webster

Opposite:
ALAN REVERE
Fold, 2003
Photo by Barry Blau

Library of Congress Cataloging-in-Publication Data

1000 rings : inspiring adornments for the hand / editor, Marthe Le Van ;
introduction by Robert Ebendorf.
   p. cm.
  Includes index.
  ISBN 1-57990-508-0 (pbk.)
 1. Jewelry making. 2. Rings. I. Le Van, Marthe.
TT212.A17 2004
739.27'82--dc22

                             2004001147

10 9 8 7 6 5 4

Published by Lark Books, a division of
Sterling Publishing Co., Inc.
387 Park Avenue South, New York, N.Y. 10016

© 2004, Lark Books

Distributed in Canada by Sterling Publishing,
c/o Canadian Manda Group, 165 Dufferin Street
Toronto, Ontario, Canada M6K 3H6

Distributed in the U.K. by Guild of Master Craftsman Publications Ltd.,
Castle Place, 166 High Street, Lewes, East Sussex, England BN7 1XU
Tel: (+ 44) 1273 477374, Fax: (+ 44) 1273 478606
E-mail: pubs@thegmcgroup.com; Web: www.gmcpublications.com

Distributed in Australia by Capricorn Link (Australia) Pty Ltd.,
P.O. Box 704, Windsor, NSW 2756 Australia

The written instructions, photographs, designs, patterns, and projects in this volume are intended for the personal use of the reader and may be reproduced for that purpose only. Any other use, especially commercial use, is forbidden under law without written permission of the copyright holder.

Every effort has been made to ensure that all the information in this book is accurate. However, due to differing conditions, tools, and individual skills, the publisher cannot be responsible for any injuries, losses, and other damages that may result from the use of the information in this book.

If you have questions or comments about this book, please contact:
Lark Books, 67 Broadway, Asheville, NC 28801, (828) 253-0467

Manufactured in China

ISBN 1-57990-508-0

For information about custom editions, special sales, premium and corporate purchases, please contact Sterling Special Sales Department at 800-805-5489 or specialsales@sterlingpub.com.

C O N T E N T S

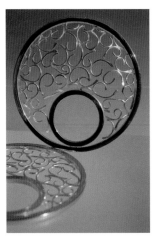

NOEL ARONOV
Swoop Ring, 1995
KIM BUCK
Solitaire Ring, 2001
SARA CILIA
Domed Ring 2, 2003

INTRODUCTION

The ring is universal. You can gaze at Saturn's rings, count a tree's rings, box in a ring, even blow smoke rings. But the subject here is one of a ring's most compelling forms: jewelry.

Whether a plain circle or a fancy frill, the ring as jewelry has many associations and makes many powerful statements. To the wearer and the observer alike, it can symbolize a variety of states and qualities: love and marriage, authority and station, accomplishment, familial bonds, or even moods. It can evoke a memory; transmit a message; signal a rite of passage; symbolize social, political, or religious affiliation; advertise status; and express personal style. A ring also can be pure adornment. Fun. Vanity.

Artists throughout history have energetically pursued creative ornamentation for the hand. Today's ring makers are more prolific than ever before, exploring both traditional forms and avant garde expressions. This book is a visual feast of contemporary ring design. In it you'll find images that capture the extraordinary imagination, craftsmanship, and originality of international artists at the top of their field. From a riot of precisely cut, polished, and set stones to a simple ribbon woven around the fingers, the stylistic variety of the rings is enormous. Some rings will astound you with their modest yet powerful forms. Others will stimulate, perhaps even agitate, you with their unorthodox fashion. Rings can be boisterous or quiet, husky or ethereal, meticulous or improvised. They're a compact platform on which some artists even tell stories or create poetic visual metaphors. In total, this collection demonstrates the diversity of the modern ring and ring makers, and it is my great honor and delight to present it to you.

Rings most often are designed to be displayed on the hand and engage the finger. The hand is a dynamic extremity that is seldom static. Along with the mouth and eyes, the hand is an articulate body part that can be said to actually "talk." As such, it is continually on display, speaking its own language, moving, gesturing, communicating with the world. This strength makes the hand a particularly attractive and challenging site for adornment, and there are limitless ways for the maker, the wearer, and the viewer to converse.

A ring can be much more than a band that houses a single finger. Many jewelers have ventured beyond this barrier and fashioned rings to be worn on several fingers simultaneously. Some rings are intended to be viewed from the underside of the hand, furnishing the wearer with a secret to reveal. Other rings require the wearer to play an active role and hold the ring in place by consciously squeezing a fist or fingers. Some pieces are meant to be worn across the tips of the fingers rather than slid down to their base. The more abstract a ring becomes, the more it seems to emphasize form over function. The most extreme examples aren't even intended to be worn—they appear fashioned in a garden, growing in a tomato, or embedded in the hot asphalt of a street.

Some artists sculpt rings from opulent and costly materials—gold, platinum, diamonds, gemstones—while others realize the innate beauty of found objects and manmade materials such as plastics, fibers, wood, and bone. The techniques they employ are equally vast. Rings are woven, kiln fired, carved, poured, forged, whittled, extruded, flameworked, cold connected, and more. Jewelers are also reviving and reinterpreting ancient methods once considered passé—granulation, niello, lost wax casting, enameling, inlay, kum-boo. Within the field, such classical practices can coexist and even synthesize with modern technology, producing remarkable results.

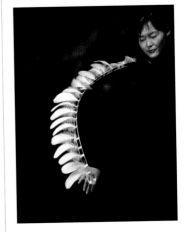

As all artists, ring makers are in a state of perpetual growth. Sharing information with others, especially in this age of electronic communication, is easier and more fruitful than ever before. Cultural exchanges are taking place that will affect the future aesthetics of jewelry on a truly global scale. Artists are gaining an appreciation for the world's ring makers, and in doing so, enriching their own efforts. This vibrant cross-pollination is being characterized by an almost osmotic transfer of styles, methodologies, materials, and even ways of seeing between makers. Like its unending form, the ring's future is infinite and its interpretation inexhaustible. Jurying this collection was a humbling, exciting, challenging, and joyful experience. I'm proud to be a part of the history of the ring, and I'm proud to be a part of a field that celebrates excellence, nurtures leadership, and attracts public interest with marvelous energy.

ROBERT W. EBENDORF

E. ELIZABETH PETERS
Spiral Wrap Ring with Amethyst, 2002
LORI TALCOTT
Mardöll II, 2002
SEO YOON CHOI
Desire, 1999

THE RINGS

MIA MALJOJOKI

Cluster Series #2, 2003

2.5 x 2.5 x 2.5 cm

18-karat gold, silver, sapphire, pearl

Photo by Dean Powell

HAROLD O'CONNOR

From the Quarry, 2002

5 x 2.5 x .7 cm

18-karat gold, silver, limestone; fabricated

Photo by artist

LOUISE NORRELL

Man's Two-Part Wedding Band, 2002

3 x 1.1 x 2.4 cm

18-karat yellow gold, 18-karat white gold,

violet sapphire; fabricated, chased, bezel set

Photo by Walker Montgomery

J. E. PATERAK

3 Rings, from the *Pod and Stamen Series*, 2000

3.2 x 1.9 cm (average)

Oxidized sterling silver, 18-karat gold, diamond,

moonstone

Photo by Robert Diamante

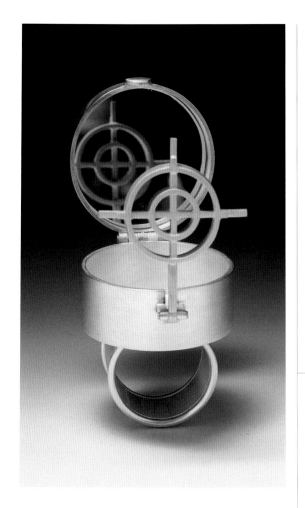

LYRA JOY FISET

Caesar's a Bridge Away, from the *Oculus Series*, 2000

6 x 6.4 cm

Silver, bronze; cast, fabricated

Photo by Phil Poirier

TARA STEPHENSON

Sight #3, 1997

5.7 x 2.5 x 2.5 cm

Sterling silver, mirror;

fabricated, soldered, cast

Photo by Dennis Nahabetian

MELANIE SEILER

Pair of Rings, 2003

3.5 x 3 x 2.5 cm

Silver, graphite; wax modeled, cast

Photo by Samuel Durling

ERIN TRACY

Invitation, 2002

5 x 4.5 x 3 cm

Sterling silver, acrylic

Photo by artist

HILDE LEISS

Ring, 2001

9 x 5 x 2.7 cm

Sterling silver, quartz crystal

Courtesy of Andora Gallery, Carefree, Arizona

Photo by Studio Miko

KATHRYN WARDILL

Tall Bead Rings (three from a series of 18), 2001

10 x 5 x 3 cm

Sterling silver, glass; hand carved, wax cast,

fabricated, lampworked

Photo by artist

MICHELLE NICOLE BEATRICE

Push Pin Ring, 2002

.9 x 2.5 x 2.5 cm

Sterling silver, push pin heads;

cast, soldered, drilled, assembled

Photo by Robin Kraft

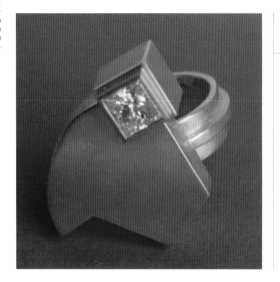

JAN WEHRENS

Ring, 2002

3 x 2.5 x 3 cm

Gold, diamond

Photo by artist

CHRISTA LÜHTJE

Ring, 2002

2.6 x 1.2 cm

22-karat gold

Photo by Eva Jünger

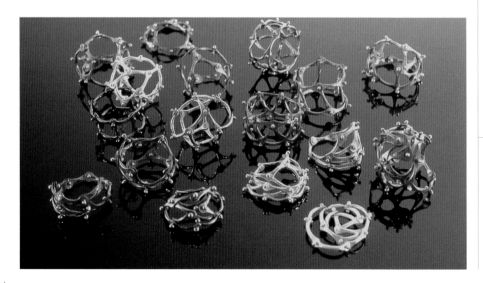

KRISTINE BOLHUIS

Structural Ring Studies, 2002

2.5 x 2.5 x 2.5 cm (each)

Sterling silver, 18-karat gold,

14-karat gold, brass; hand

constructed, hand forged

Photo by artist

RICHARD MAWDSLEY

Ring, 1981

2.5 x 1.9 x 1.9 cm

14-karat gold, amethyst; fabricated

Photo by artist

LISA FIDLER

4 Rings, 2002

2.5 cm in diameter (each)

Sterling silver, 18-karat gold,

glass; hand constructed

Photo by Hap Sakwa

STEVEN GOODMAN

2 Rings, 2002
3.2 x 3.2 x 1.9 cm
Sterling silver, fossilized
mammoth and mastodon
ivory; fabricated, inlaid
Photo by Susan Jackson

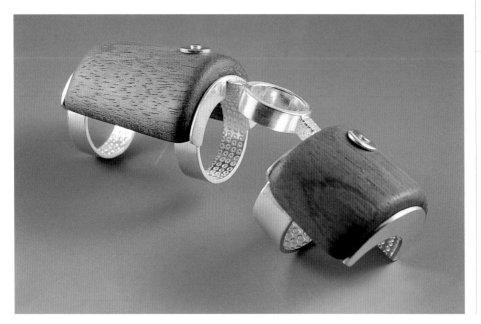

DANIEL HUYNH

Ring for a Broken Finger II, 2003
7.6 x 5 x 5 cm
Sterling silver, rosewood;
fabricated, chased, carved
Photo by artist

JU-HYUN LEE

Ring, 2003

6.5 x 3 x 2.7 cm

Sterling silver

Photo by Myung-Wook Huh

(Studio Munch)

ALOIS BAUER

Ring, 1997

2.6 x 2.4 x .4 cm

18-karat gold

Photos by Pia Odorizzi

ANGELA GLEASON

Halo for St. Anne: Patroness of Young Writers;
Invoked Against Anti-Semites, 2001

4.1 x 3.8 x .8 cm

Sterling silver, pencils, eraser; fabricated

Photo by Hap Sakwa

OTTO KÜNZLI

Faceless, 1993

3.5 x 3.5 x .8 cm

Gold; cast

Photo by artist

HERMANN JÜNGER

Helen's Ring, 1990

Gold, opal, chrysoprase, emerald,

tourmaline, rough diamond, sapphire

Collection of the Museum of Fine Arts, Houston, Texas

Photo by Eva Jünger

ROBERT W. EBENDORF

Red Finger Ring, 2003

3.2 x 1.9 cm

Red glass, 18-karat gold, beach

glass, silver; constructed

Photo by artist

19

TODD REED

Grouping of Diamond Rings, 2003

Various dimensions

18-karat yellow gold, 22-karat yellow gold,

18-karat palladium white gold, sterling silver,

cut diamonds, natural uncut diamond cubes,

mackles, and octahedrons; hand forged,

fabricated, brushed finish

Photo by Azad

PAMELA ARGENTIERI

Blossom Ring IV, 2003

3.2 x 1.9 x 1.9 cm

Sterling silver, fine silver, enamel,

24-karat gold foil; cast, fabricated

Photo by Matthew Hollern

CLAUDIO PINO

Extravaganza Ring, 2003
1.3 x 4.4 x 1.9 cm
18-karat red gold,
sterling silver, citrines, opal
Photo by Philomène Longpré

YUKA SAITO

Untitled, 2001
3.5 x 3 x 3 cm
18-karat gold, beryl, mandarin
garnet; constructed
Courtesy of Mobilia Gallery,
Cambridge, Massachusetts
Photo by artist

GERD ROTHMANN
Signet Ring, 1987
2.8 x 2.4 x 1.3 cm
Gold; finger printed
Photo by Wilfried Petzi

JIM COTTER
Concrete and Pearl Ring, 2001
3.8 x 3 x 1.3 cm
Concrete, 14-karat yellow gold, mabe pearl
Photo by Schempf

JANE BOWDEN
Woven Ring, 1998
5 x 4 x 2.5 cm
Sterling silver, 18-karat
green gold, 24-karat gold;
hand fabricated, woven
Photo by Grant Hancock

I love making pieces that provoke questions. Is that a ring? How can you wear that? How did you make that?

Jane Bowden

ANNEKE SCHAT

Lente Maan (Spring Moon), 1991

8.8 x 3.2 x 4.9 cm

18-karat gold, moonstone

Photo by Pim Kielen

● **This ring substitutes the wearer's skin in place of the traditional gemstone for inspection, possibly introspection.**

Sondra Sherman

SONDRA SHERMAN

Skin: 4 Fingers, 2001

3 x 5.6 x 1.9 cm

Oxidized silver, optical lens; constructed

Photo by artist

NANCY BONNEMA

White Ring, 2002

2.5 cm in diameter

Copper, enamel, beads, sterling silver

Photo by Douglas Yaple

ESTHER HELÉN SLAGSVOLD

Container for Memories No. II, 2002

3.4 x 2.1 x 1.2 cm

Silver, ebony; hand carved, painted

Photo by artist

CHRISTOPH SCHULZ

Faltring (Fold Ring), 2002

3.3 x 4.5 x .9 cm

Titanium, diamond; tension set

Photo by Dirk Krähmer

ELIZABETH BONE

Moon Ring, 2001

6 cm wide

Silver; fabricated

Photo by Joël Degen

Material and process guided by order, balance, and a modernist influence form the basis for my work. I value clean lines, geometric forms, and honesty in the use of materials. My working vocabulary contains many visual references to mechanical production, though this belies the fact that the pieces are produced entirely by hand: sawing, filing, shaping, and coaxing, striving for precision and purity. This is what motivates me.

Elizabeth Bone

MIZUKO YAMADA

Silver Ring, 2003

4.5 x 7 x 2.5 cm

Silver; hammered, soldered

Photo by Toshihide Kajihara

TOM FERRERO

Chalice Ring, Black, 2002

3.8 x 5 x 2.5 cm

Sterling silver, 22-karat gold;

fabricated, stamped

Photo by Dan Neuburger

HATTIE SANDERSON

Precious Metal Clay Ring, 2003

2.5 x 2.5 x 2.5 cm

Precious metal clay, trillion cut

olivine cubic zirconia, patina;

hand formed, kiln fired

Photo by artist

ERIK TIDÄNG

Jetengine, 2003

3.5 x 3 x 5 cm

Silver

Photo by artist

TAS KERLEY

His & Hers Chaos Rings, 2003

2.2 x .6 x .2 cm (left); 2.1 x .4 x .2 cm (right)

High-carbon steel, nickel, 14-karat pink gold;

forge welded, forged, machined, alloyed, soldered

Photo by Pascal Veyradier

CHRISTOPH SCHULZ

Schichtring (Layer Ring), 1999

2.5 x 2.5 x 1.2 cm

18-karat gold, titanium,

tantalum; pinned, soldered

Photo by Dirk Krähmer

CARRIE PERKINS

Chewed Up and Spit Out Series, 2001

5 x 5 x .6 cm

Sterling silver, bubble gum; fabricated

Photo by Robly A. Glover

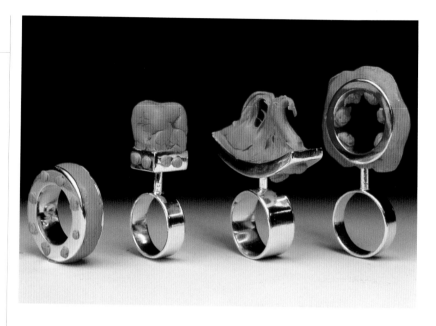

SIGURD BRONGER

Ring, 2000

7 x 2 cm (ring); 25 cm (balloon diameter)

Steel, silver, brass, balloon

Photos by artist

TARA STEPHENSON

Continuous Removal, 1997–1998

5 x 2.5 x 2.5 cm

Sterling silver, mirror, pink eraser;

fabricated, soldered, bezel set

Photo by Dennis Nahabetian

RENÉE ZETTLE-STERLING

Survival Tip #11, 2000

Variable dimensions

Silver, nickel, chalkboard,

chalk, eraser; fabricated

Photos by David Smith

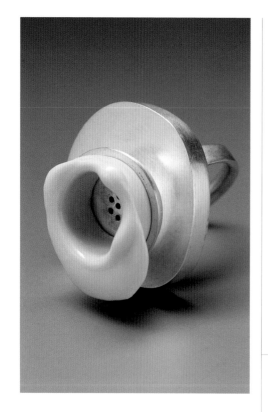

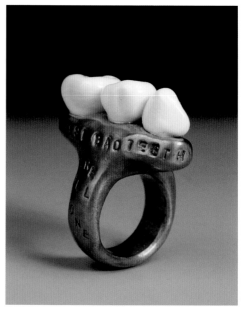

JENNIFER METTLEN NOLAN

Don't Worry Hun, Those Bad Teeth

Are All Gone!, 2003

6.4 x 6.4 x 6.4 cm

Glass, copper; lampworked, cast

Photo by Robly A. Glover

KATJA PRINS

Untitled, 2002

3 x 3.5 x 4 cm

Silver, porcelain

Photo by Eddo Hartmann

DANIEL KRUGER
Untitled, 2003
5 x 4 x 5 cm
Sterling silver, coral,
malachite; constructed
Photo by Thilo Haertlein

ROSS LUNZ
The Pursuit of Happiness, 2001
15.2 x 6.9 x 6.4 cm
Plastic found objects, rubber found objects, epoxy resin
Photo by artist

JAISY HANLON
Three Rings, from the
Preservation Series, 2002
5 x 3.8 cm (left); 9.5 x 2.5 cm (center);
6.4 x 4.4 cm (right)
Oxidized silver, found object, paint, steel
wire, Protea bristles, copper pod, lichen,
beeswax; electroformed, fabricated
Photo by Gina Rymarcsuk

ANN A. LALIK

East Meets West, 2002

3.5 x 2.8 x 3.2 cm

New Jersey seashell, Sedona rock,

sterling silver, 14-karat yellow gold;

reticulated, fabricated

Photo by Hub Willson

JONI JOHNSON

Below, from the series *Preposition Rings*, 2002

3.1 x 3.8 x 2.5 cm

18-karat yellow gold, clear quartz; scored,

folded, soldered, hand faceted, prong set

Photo by James Beards Photography

KAROL WEISSLECHNER

Tatry, 2002

6 x 6 x 5.5 cm

Silver, granite, gold leaf, patina

Photo by Pavol Janek

C. JAMES MEYER

Rock Ring, 1994

3.2 x 2.5 x 1.9 cm

18-karat green gold, platinum,

diamond, found rock; fabricated

Photo by Taylor Dabney

● **Bridges fascinate me because they are beautiful, functional, and usually accompanied by a natural phenomenon such as a body of water. I love the juxtaposition of architectural or manmade beauty and natural beauty.**

Hilary Hachey

HILARY HACHEY

Howard Street Bridge, 2002

4.4 x 3.8 x 1 cm

Sterling silver, sandpaper, patina; hand fabricated

Photo by Hap Sakwa

TORE SVENSSON

Ring, 2002

4 x 3 x .1 cm

Steel; silver-plated, etched, burned with linseed oil

Photo by Anders Jirås

ALBERTO ZORZI

The Town Ring, 2002

5 x 3 x 2.5 cm

18-karat gold

Photo by Massimo Sormonta

GIORGIO CECCHETTO

Alfa 2, 2002

5 x 2 x 1.5 cm

18-karat yellow gold, patina;

forged, bent, soldered, scratched

Photo by Richard Khoury

KATHRYN WARDILL

Crystal Ring Series, 2000

4 x 3 x 3 cm

Sterling silver, pure gold;

hand fabricated

Photo by artist

TIFFANY PARBS

From the Displacement Series, 2003

1.9 x 1.9 x 3 cm (left);

2.2 x 2.2 x 2.4 cm (right)

Sterling silver, camera lens; fabricated

Photos by Greg Harris

JOËL DEGEN

2 Rings, 2000

2.2 x 1 x .3 cm (each)

18-karat yellow gold, stainless

steel, titanium; riveted

Photo by artist

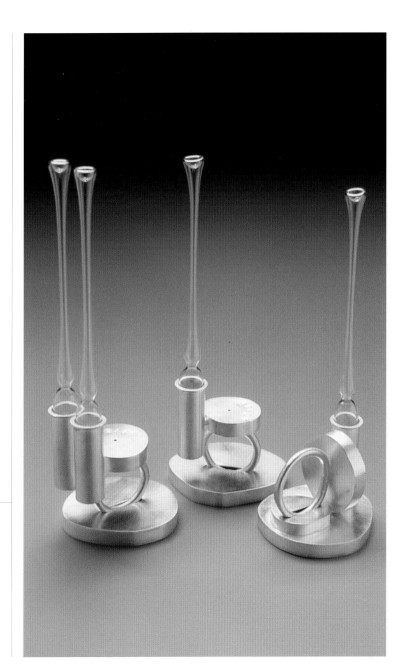

KATJA PRINS
Untitled, 2002
8 x 3.5 x 3.5 cm (each)
Silver, ampoule
Photo by Eddo Hartmann

CLAUDETTE HARDY-PILON

Ring, 2000

2.1 x 2.5 x 1 cm

Sterling silver, 18-karat gold;

lost wax cast, constructed

Photo by Daniel Roussel for Centre

de Documentation Yvan Boulerice

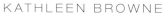

KATHLEEN BROWNE

Rattle, 2000

5 x 2.5 x 2.5 cm

Fine silver, sterling silver, 24-karat gold,

18-karat gold, precious metal clay;

cast, fabricated

Photo by artist

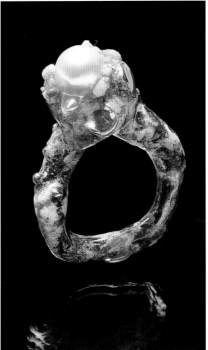

SHARI PIERCE

Ring, 2000

5 x 17.8 cm

Sterling silver; forged

Photo by artist

TOMOMI ARATA

Treasures from Under the Sea, 2003

3.8 x 2.7 x 1.5 cm

Silver, enamel, sand, pearl; hand cast

Photo by Minoru Hashimoto

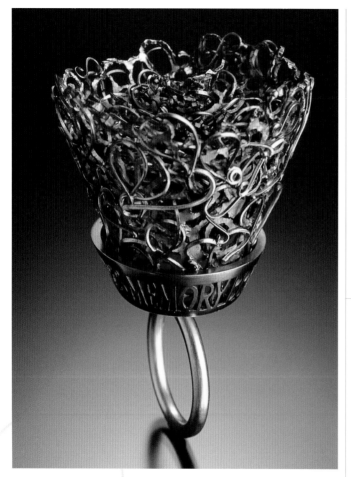

SHARON PORTELANCE

Memory Breathes #1, 2003

6.9 x 2.8 x 2.8 cm

Sterling silver, 22-karat gold, 18-karat gold, enamel; fabricated

Photos by Robert Diamante

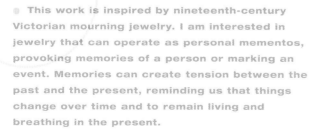

This work is inspired by nineteenth-century Victorian mourning jewelry. I am interested in jewelry that can operate as personal mementos, provoking memories of a person or marking an event. Memories can create tension between the past and the present, reminding us that things change over time and to remain living and breathing in the present.

Sharon Portelance

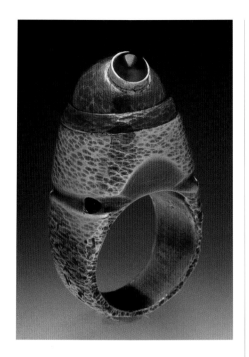

This ring series is a result of my wish to use semiprecious translucent beads in an unconventional way, setting them rather than stringing them.

Daphne Krinos

WILEY F. JACKSON

Untitled, 2002

4.5 x 1.7 x 1.5 cm

Sterling silver, garnet, brass ball bearing, copper, stainless steel; cast, fabricated

Photo by Leslie Bauer

DAPHNE KRINOS

Ring 1, 2002

3 x 1.2 x .5 cm

Silver, 18-karat gold, lemon citrine bead

Photo by Joël Degen

RIAN de JONG

Coral Garden (two-finger ring), 1997

3 x 4.5 x 2.5 cm

Wood, coral, silver

Photo by artist

PETER HOOGEBOOM

Friendship Rings (set), 1995

4 x 2.8 x 2 cm (each)

Silver, glazed ceramics

Photo by Henni van Beek

ELIZABETH BONE

Ring, 1997

5 x 3 x .6 cm

Silver, 22-karat gold leaf;

cast, fabricated

Photo by Joël Degen

SUSAN MAY

Tall Ring, 2002

4 x 2.5 x 1.2 cm

18-karat gold; forged

Photo by Joël Degen

CHRISTA LÜHTJE

Ring, 2002

2.2 x 1.5 cm

22-karat gold, 12-karat

palladium gold; forged

Photo by Eva Jünger

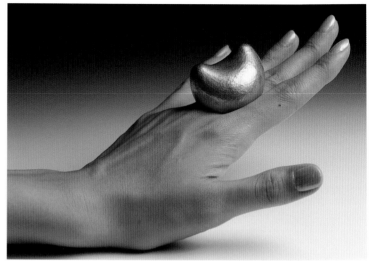

ROB JACKSON

Duomo, 1994

3.8 x 2.5 x 2.5 cm

Silver, 20-karat gold, topaz, garnets,

cameo shell; lost wax cast, fabricated,

carved, bezel set, tube set

Photo by artist

MIZUKO YAMADA

Tactile Ring, 2000

4 x 4.5 x 4.5 cm

Silver; hammered, soldered, mercury gilded

Photo by Toshihide Kajihara

ANIKA SMULOVITZ

Herbarium Specimen Rings, 2002

7.6 x 1.9 x 1.9 cm (each)

Sterling silver, glass, specimens;

fabricated

Photo by artist

JULIE BROOKS PRICE

Two of a Kind—Female, 2001

3.8 x 3.8 x 3.5 cm

Sterling silver, copper, limoges

enamel, decals; fabricated

Photo by Scott McMahon

LORI MÜLLER

Duomo, 2003

5.1 x 2.3 x 2 cm

Sterling silver, garnet cabochon, patina; hollow

form constructed, textured, hinged, bezel set

Photo by Lauch McKenzie

JUDY WENIG-HORSWELL

Trophy Ring IV, 2003

5 x 3.2 x 1.9 cm

Sterling silver; lost wax cast

Photo by Eric A. Nisly

BARBARA WALTER

Bearings, 1999–2000

3.8 x 2.5 x 2.5 cm (each)

Sterling silver, fine silver, gold, compass, level, wood; cast, fabricated

Photos by artist

● *Bearings* is a series about how we identify our place in the environment. These rings are based on familiar instruments used to read some aspect of our surroundings: horizontal, vertical, time, and direction. The use of bears is for the pun and as a reference to nature. All of these rings are kinetic. The spherical rings collapse to be worn.

Barbara Walter

BROCK T. BURNELL

Specimen 1, 2002

4 x 3.3 x 1.2 cm

Sterling silver, glass, liquid; fabricated

Photo by artist

KATHLEEN BAILEY

Bling, Bling, 2003

7 x 4 x 4 cm

Sugar crystals, silver, copper,
gold; electroformed, plated

Photo by Joël Degen

HEE-SEUNG KOH

Piling-up 1, 2003

4.4 x 3 x 1.7 cm

Sterling silver, 24-karat gold,

ivory, quartz, bead, copper

Photos by Kwang-Chun Park

(KC Studio)

SERENA VAN RENSSELAER

Isadora Ring, from *The Couture Feather Collection*, 2002

10.2 x 6.4 x 5 cm

Sterling silver, 18-karat gold,

freshwater pearls, ostrich feathers

Photo by Danielle Cleary

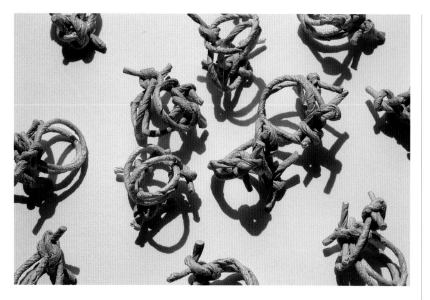

MARI ISHIKAWA

En Ring, 2002

2.5 x 4 x 3 cm

Sterling silver; cast

Photo by Frank Vetter

SANDRA GILES

Stock Pot Ring, from the
Culinary Series, 2003

5 x 3.2 x 2.5 cm

Sterling silver, fine silver;
hollow constructed, granulated

Photo by artist

LYRA JOY FISET

Ewok, from the *Oculus Series*, 2000

4.4 x 2.8 cm

Silver, bronze, cubic zirconia,
lucite; cast, fabricated

Photo by Phil Poirier

JOHANNA BECKER-BLACK

Front Yard, 2003

3.5 x 2.5 x 2.5 cm

Sterling silver, 22-karat gold;

fabricated, constructed

Photo by Federico Cavicchioli

GISELA KUNZ

Revolving Star, 2000–2003

4 x 3.5 x 3.5 cm

Sterling silver, revolving star anise;

cast, fabricated

Photo by Ralph Gabriner

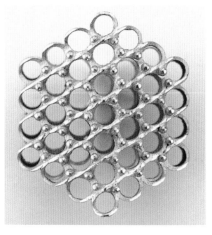

HERMANN JÜNGER

'70s Ring, 1980

Gold, opal, chrysoprase

Photo by Eva Jünger

ERICO NAGAI

Tube 1, 1996

3.4 x 2.6 x 3.2 cm

28-karat gold

Photos by George Meister

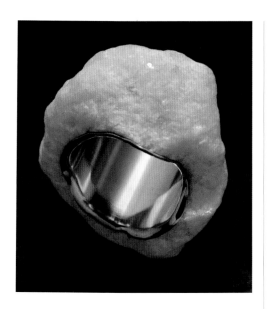

JIM COTTER

Rock Ring, 2000

3.8 x 3 x 1.6 cm

Marble, 14-karat yellow gold

Photo by R. Hedstrom

RAUL FRISNEDA and KEITH FREMON

Atlas, 2001

2.5 x 3.3 x 1.3 cm

18-karat yellow gold, white diamonds,

South Sea golden pearl; hand fabricated,

lost wax cast, burnish set

Photo by Ralph Gabriner

JAN WEHRENS

Four Rings, 2002

Various dimensions

Gold, silver

Photo by artist

ANNELI TAMMIK

Le Couple, 2001

2.5 x 2.5 x .7 cm (connected)

14-karat yellow gold,

14-karat red gold, diamonds

Photo by Priit Palomets

VICKI MASON

Triple Sprouter, 2000

3.2 x 2.5 x .9 cm

Sterling silver, nylon fiber,

hand-dyed nylon; fabricated, lathe

turned, drilled, set, tension set

Photo by Grant Hancock

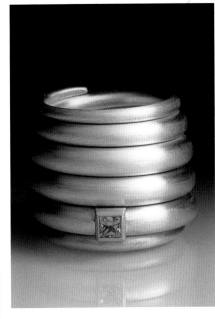

As a child growing up on the Australian gem fields, I collected tiny brightly colored chips of sapphires that sparkled on the ground after the rain. In this piece, the positioning of one golden sapphire brings the silver spiral ring to life.

Mark Nuell

MARK NUELL

Untitled, 2003

2.7 x 2.7 x 1.9 cm

Silver, 18-karat gold, yellow

sapphire; hand forged, set

Photo by Peter White

NICK MOWERS

Spinnin' Tile Ring, 2000

4.4 x 4.1 x 2.5 cm

Sterling silver, found ceramic tile;

hollow form constructed

Photo by Scott McMahon

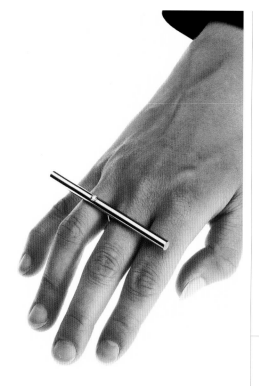

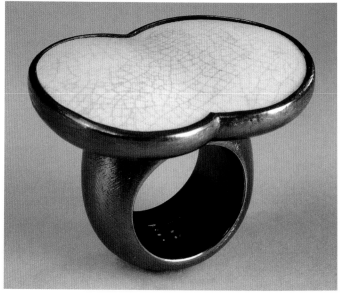

GÜNTER WERMEKES

In-Between-Finger-Ring, 1985–2001

.5 x 3 x 5.5 cm

Stainless steel; constructed

Photo by Dirk Albrecht

ROBIN QUIGLEY

Double I, 2001

4.4 x 3.8 x 3.8 cm

Silver, porcelain shard, 18-karat gold

Courtesy of Mobilia Gallery,

Cambridge, Massachusetts

Photo by Mark Johnston

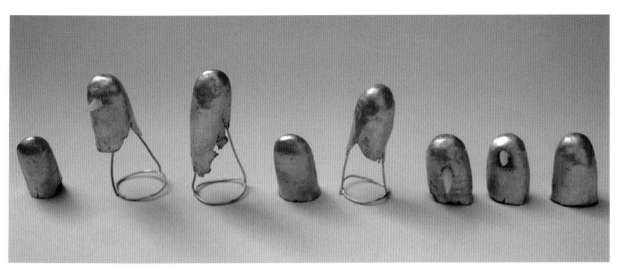

KRISTI PAAP

Communication, 1995

Various dimensions

Silver, Plexiglas®

Photo by artist

EVA I. WERNER

Sterling Silver Ring, 2002

2.6 x 2.6 x .8 cm

Sterling silver; constructed, wired, soldered

Photo by Peter White

ANGIE BOOTHROYD

Symmetry Ring (Clover), 2000

2 x 5.5 x 5.5 cm

Sterling silver; water-jet cut, milling
machine scored, soldered, finished

Photo by artist

PATRICK MARCHAL

Tikal, 1996

5.2 x 2.5 x .6 cm

18-karat gold; cut,
assembled, soldered

Photo by artist

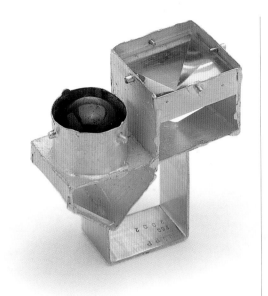

ANDREA WIPPERMANN

Untitled, 2002

3.8 x 4 x 1.3 cm

Gold, sapphire; cast

Photo by Christoph Sandig

KLAUS SPIES

Moebius, 2003

2 x 2 x .7 cm

18-karat yellow gold, Burmese rubies;

wax carved, cast, channel set

Photo by Larry Sanders

ROB JACKSON

Taper, 2000

2.5 x 2.5 x .9 cm

100-year-old hand-forged

nail, 18-karat gold

Photo by artist

ALESSIA SEMERARO

Fuoco Ottimale, 2002

3 x 3 x 2 cm

Cedar wood, resin;

constructed, burnt, coated

Photo by Ray Boom

EUN JU PARK

Ring II, 2003

5.7 x 5.6 x 2.5 cm

Sterling silver, yellow copper,

turtle back; kum-boo

Photo by Myung-Wook Huh

(Studio Munch)

CLAUDIA RINNEBERG

Spirit of Elements, 2003

3.9 x 3.4 x .7 cm

Iron, 14-karat gold; sawed, bent, drilled

Photo by Federico Cavicchioli

JULIE BROOKS PRICE

High Cotton, 2002

6.9 x 5 x 5 cm

Sterling silver, cotton bud, steel;

cast, fabricated

Photo by John Clemmer

SUSANNE KLEMM

fire and fired, 2001

4 x 2 x 1 cm (each)

Silver, varnish; forged

Courtesy of Galerie Ra,

Amsterdam, Netherlands

Photo by artist

ERIN B. GRAY

Spoon Rings (series of five), 2001

7.3 x 3.8 x .6 cm (average)

Sterling silver, epoxy resin,

pigment; formed, inlaid

Photo by Chip Schwartz

In this series, I wanted to make jewelry more functional, so I created rings with which you can eat.

Erin B. Gray

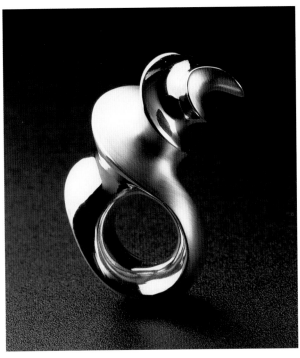

MARIO SUGA

Wing, 2003

7 x 4 x 2 cm

Silver; cast

Photo by Hiroshi SUGA

GIAMPAOLO BABETTO

Untitled, 2002

3.7 x 2.8 x 2.9 cm

18-karat yellow gold, pigment

Photo by Lorenzo Trento

This design is based on the playground equipment I climbed on as a child. Although the ring is rather large, it is durable enough to withstand daily use, allowing the wearer to play with the marbles during life's more monotonous moments.

Jesse Mathes

JESSE MATHES

Play, 2000

6.3 x 5 x 5 cm

Sterling silver, glass marbles; fabricated

Photo by Helen Shirk

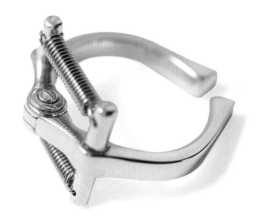

SEAN O'CONNELL

Snap Trap Ring, 2003

2.5 x 2.2 x 1.4 cm

Sterling silver, Remanium®, 18-karat gold; fabricated, riveted, lathe-wound springs

Photo by Albert Paca

CAROL WEBB

Assorted Rings, 2000

2.5 x 2.5 x 2.5 cm (each)

Copper, fine silver, black patina; photo etched

Photo by Ralph Gabriner

FLORIAN BUDDEBERG

Net Ring, 2002

5 x 3.5 cm

Silver, paint

Photo by artist

CHRISSY JAY

Twig Ring I and *Nature's Crown*, 2003

2.5 x 2.5 x 1 cm (each)

Ebony, sterling silver, 18-karat gold;

lathe turned, constructed, soldered

Photo by artist

KATJA PRINS

Untitled, 1998

1.5 x 2 x 2 cm (each)

Silver, polyurethane rubber, pearls

Photo by Gerhard Jaeger

YVONNE GALLEY-KNAPPE

Untitled, 2001

2 x 2 x 2.6 cm (each)

Sterling silver, synthetic stones

Photo by artist

JANE BOWDEN

Shake, Rattle, and Roll, 2001
3.7 x 3.7 x 1.6 cm
Sterling silver, 18-karat gold;
fabricated
Photo by Grant Hancock

KATHLEEN BAILEY

Cluster Rings, 2003
3.5 x 3.3 x 2 cm (seven rings together)
Silver, guitar string shanks; fabricated
Photo by Joël Degen

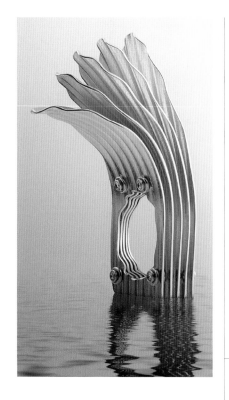

ALAN REVERE

Fold, 2003

5.7 x 2.5 x 3.2 cm

18-karat yellow gold, 14-karat
red gold, platinum, diamonds;
corrugated, fabricated
Photo by Barry Blau

NATHALIE GOULIART

Bague à Essayer (The Ring to Wear), 2002

5.4 x 8.4 x 1.4 cm

Gold, nickel silver; cut, laminated,
curved, riveted, plated
Photo by Aline Princet

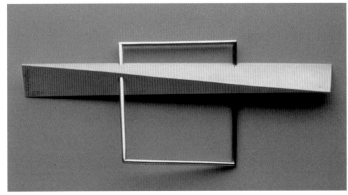

VISINTIN GRAZIANO

Ring, 1985

3 x 7.2 cm

Yellow gold, white gold

Photo by Lorenzo Trento

STEFANO MARCHETTI

Untitled, 1995

2.5 x 2.5 x 1.5 cm

Gold; mokume gane, parquetry

Photo by Roberto Sordi

BRUCE CLARK

Scratch That Itch: Silver Threads and
Golden Needles, 2003

7.6 x 2.5 x .3 cm (each)

Mesquite thorns, brass, rubber, metal leaf

Photo by Robin Stancliff

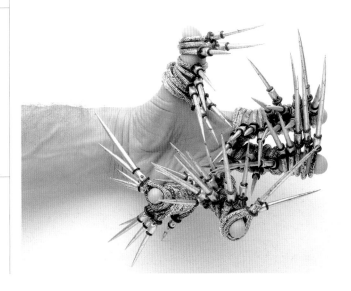

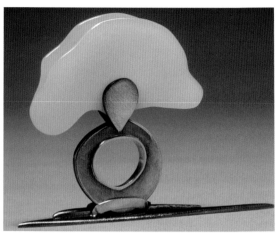

SUZANNE AMENDOLARA

Papavar, 2003

6.4 x 8.2 x .6 cm

Sterling silver, 18-karat gold, Plexiglas®,

22-karat gold; mokume gane, forged,

fabricated, constructed

Photo by artist

PEI CHI HUNG

Flower Rings, 2003

10 x 10 x 5 cm (each)

Silver, brass, copper, enamel,

gold leaf, fabric; fabricated

Photo by Kuen Lung Tsai

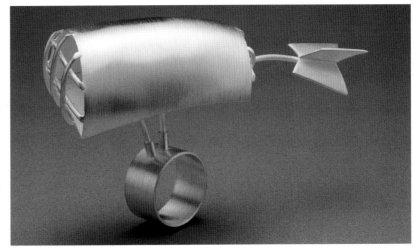

RAINER HERRMANN

Leibniz Ring, 2001

3 x 3.1 x .6 cm

18-karat gold, platinum,

aquamarine; hollow constructed

Photo by Rainer Schäle

JOON HEE KIM

Fly II, 2003

5.5 x 6.5 x 2.5 cm

Sterling silver

Photo by Myung-Wook Huh (Studio Munch)

GEORG DOBLER

Crystal-Rock-Rings, 1993–1999

Various dimensions

Rough aquamarine, rock crystal,

22-karat gold; cut, inlaid

Photo by artist

CATHY CHOTARD

Untitled, 2003

1.6 x 2.4 cm

Gold, nylon thread

Photo by artist

VISINTIN GRAZIANO

Rings, 2000

1.8 x 1.5 cm (left);

1.8 x 1.2 cm (right)

Yellow gold, white gold, niello

Photo by Lorenzo Trento

SARA WASHBUSH

Wedding Bands, 2003

2.1 x .5 x 2.1 cm (left); 1.7 x .5 x 1.7 cm (right)

14-karat yellow gold, 14-karat rose gold,

18-karat yellow gold; fabricated

Photo by artist

For small objects such as wedding bands, I choose subtle materials and forms. With these rings, the rose gold and the yellow gold form the visible band, while the bright 18-karat gold lining is solely for the bride and groom. It is a reminder that what they have together is precious.

Sara Washbush

VISINTIN GRAZIANO

Rings, 1981

2.5 x 3 cm (left); 2.6 x 3 cm (right)

Yellow gold

Photo by Lorenzo Trento

DAVID NELSON

Deco Ring, 2000

2.9 x 1.8 x .8 cm

14-karat gold, sterling silver,

cat's eye moonstone; fabricated,

riveted, stepped-bezel set

Photo by Barry J. Blau

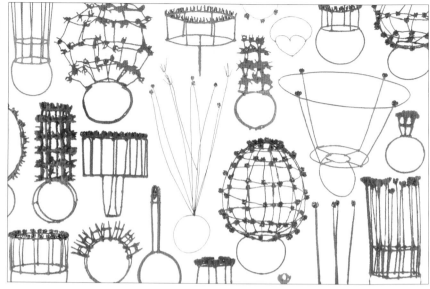

BETTINA DITTLMANN

Ringchen, 2001–2003

.1 x 2.3 x 2.7 cm to 7.4 x 6 x 6 cm

Iron wire, garnet, pyrite, enamel; soldered, bezel set

Photos by Dittlmann/Jank

YUKI MURATA

Orb, 2002

3.8 x 2.8 x 2.2 cm (each)

White earthenware;

slip cast, fired, glazed

Photo by artist

ROBLY A. GLOVER

K9-1, 2003

7.6 x 6.4 x 6.4 cm

Rubber, sterling silver;

constructed

Photo by artist

KIKKAN HULTHÉN

Lucia Ring, 2001

3.8 x 395 x .2 cm

Polyester; sewn

Photo by artist

In Sweden we celebrate St. Lucia Day on the 13th of December. In the image of Lucia, girls style themselves in a plain white dress with long red ribbons hanging in front. They wear a crown of light and fold their hands as if praying. Being chosen to be Lucia is an honor. The girl gets everyone's attention, which can make her nervous, causing her palms to sweat and hands to shake. In this jewelry I wanted to help keep Lucia's hands together, so I made her belt into a ring for all fingers.

Kikkan Hulthén

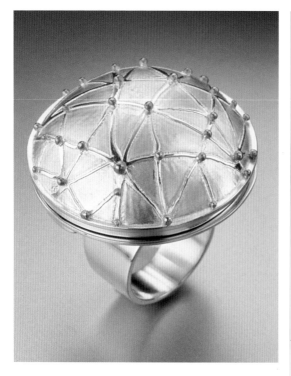

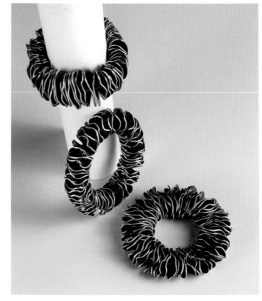

BIBA SCHUTZ

Crinkle Rings, 2002

Various dimensions

Oxidized sterling silver; stretched,
manipulated, drilled, fitted, soldered

Photo by Ron Boszko

CAROLINE LINDHOLM

Inner Beauty, 1999

4.5 x 3.5 cm

Silver, 22-karat gold beads, mirror,
pearls; constructed, etched, latticed

Photos by Hans Bjurling

In my jewelry, I work with one single element, a polygon star-formed ring. It varies in size and number of edges, and acts as a kind of module in a system with apparently infinite possibilities. I research both stable and unstable stellated structures to make jewelry that, though very tied to an absolute system, can be experienced as vividly vibrating organisms with many possibilities and associations.

Kirsten Clausager

KIRSTEN CLAUSAGER

Rings, 2002

2 x 2 x 2 cm

18-karat gold, silver, diamond

Photo by Ole Akhøj

SERGEY JIVETIN

Tethered Volumes Ring, 2001

2.5 x 2.5 x 1.3 cm

Nickel titanium wire,

18-karat gold; woven

Photo by artist

SHAHASP VALENTINE

Organic Ring #21, 2002

3.2 x 2.5 x 1.6 cm

Fine silver, precious metal clay, black pearl;

hand formed, fired, hand finished

Photo by Hap Sakwa

SANDRA ENTERLINE

Pierced Ring Series, 2000

3.8 x 2.5 x 2.5 cm (each)

Oxidized sterling silver, 22-karat gold;

hand fabricated, perforated

Photo by Mark Johann

LORI TALCOTT

Winter Pod Ring, 2002

8.9 x 3.8 x 1.3 cm

Silver, Lucite®, pearls; fabricated

Photo by Douglas Yaple

NOON MITCHELHILL

Rings, 2001

3 x 5 x 1 cm (each)

Sterling silver, fine silver; oxidized,

hand fabricated, cast

Photo by Joël Degen

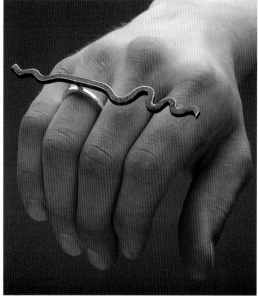

VELETA VANCZA

Menarche, 1999

2.5 x 2.2 x 2.2 cm

Sterling silver, rubber stamp, Delrin®,

ink pad; fabricated, chased

Photo by Robert Storm, Storm Photo

PATRICK PERRY

Stacked #3, 2003

3 x .3 x 10.5 cm

Sterling silver, steel

Photo by Drew Gilbert

AKIKO BAN

Untitled, 2002

2.3 x 3.5 x 3.5 cm

Shakudo, 18-karat yellow gold

Photo by Federico Cavicchioli

PAOLO MARCOLONGO

Rings, 2003

2.2 x 1.4 x 1.4 cm (each)

18-karat gold, glass, quartz

Photo by Giustino Chemello

LEZLIE JANE

A Bird in Hand..., 2003

5 x 4.4 x 3.4 cm

Lead crystal; kiln cast

Photo by Lynn Thompson

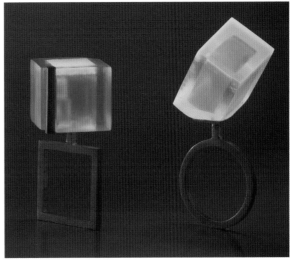

KAORI WATANABE

Tikki, Tikki..., 2003

3.7 x 2.2 x 2 cm (left); 4.8 x 2.3 x 2 cm (right)

Florescent Plexiglas®, silver; sanded

Photo by Federico Cavicchioli

SARAH CRAWFORD

Propelly, 2003

4.5 x 2.4 x .7 cm

Nylon, acrylic, silver; dyed,

constructed, joined

Photo by R. Stroud

Movement, surprise, and a sense of animation are all essential qualities I try to incorporate into each piece. Using colorful hand-knit wire I hope to illustrate these playful qualities through lightweight flexible forms that spring to life with the body in motion.

Reina Mia Brill

REINA MIA BRILL

Giddey Up (double ring), 2000

8.9 x 11.4 x 2.5 cm

Coated copper wire; hand knit

Photo by artist

SHELLEY NORTON

Untitled, 2002

37 x 3.5 x 3.5 cm

Plastic bags; cut, hand knitted, constructed

Photo by John Collie

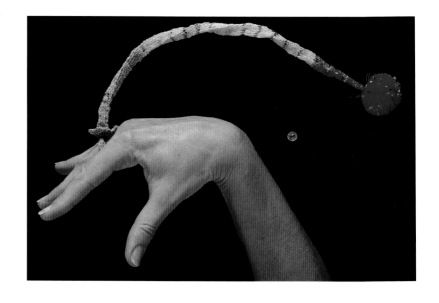

PATRICK MARCHAL

Hand Kissing, 2001

5.5 x 8 x 2.5 cm

Silver, titanium, resin; matrix cut, assembled,

soldered, electroanodized surface

Photo by Paul Louis

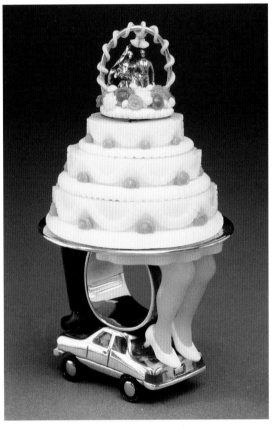

BARBARA WALTER

Wedding Bells Ring Toy, 1985

6.4 x 3.8 cm

Sterling silver, brass, plastic;

cast, fabricated, carved, turned

Photo by artist

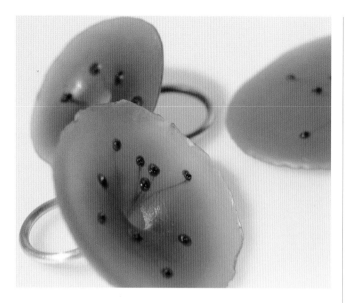

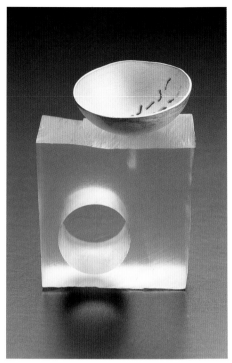

ELA BAUER

Rings, 2001

3.5 x 3.5 cm to 4.5 x 4.5 cm

Latex rubber, Teflon ® thread, silver;

strung, burnt

Photo by artist

AKIKO BAN

The Light, 2000

3 x 3 x 2 cm

Sterling silver, Perspex™

Photo by Federico Cavicchioli

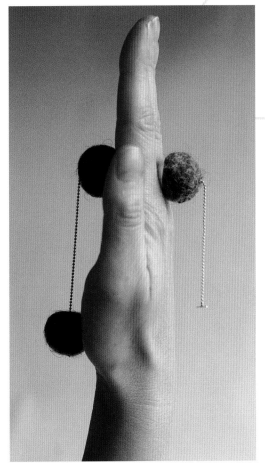

> I want the
> ring to be
> more than just
> an attachment
> to the body;
> I want it to
> be part of the
> body. It needs
> to work both
> ways, talking
> to the viewer
> but through
> the wearer.
>
> Catarina Hällzon

KAREN McCREARY

Morning Glory Ring, 2000

3.8 x 2.5 x 2.2 cm

Sterling silver, acrylic, 22-karat gold leaf;

fabricated, carved

Photo by artist

CATARINA HÄLLZON

Wanna Play?, 2002

15 x 2 x 2 cm

Wool, silver

Photo by artist

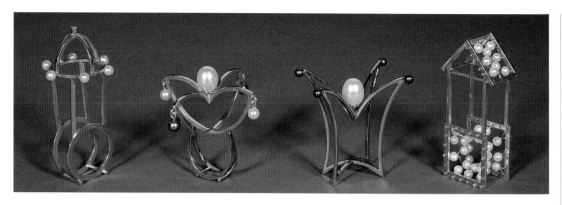

NICOLE JACQUARD

Flower & Architectural Rings, 2002

4.4 x 4.4 x 5 cm (detail)

18-karat white gold, 18-karat yellow gold, pearls,

diamond, monofilament; hand fabricated

Photos by Thomas Madden

EILEEN GERSTEIN

Domed Kum-boo Series, 1999

Various dimensions

Sterling silver, fine silver, 24-karat

gold; fabricated, kum-boo

Photo by Don Felton

I imagine that the owner of this ring travels extensively, often by sea. *Voyage* has a steady and direct presence.

D. X. Ross

E. ELIZABETH PETERS

Spiral Wrap Ring with Amethyst, 2002

2.9 x 5.1 x 3.8 cm

18-karat gold, rough cut amethyst;

hand fabricated

Photo by Petr Weigl

D. X. ROSS

Voyage, from the *Mystical Rings* series, 1985

3.2 x 1.9 x 3.2 cm

Sterling silver, gemstones, 18-karat gold,

22-karat gold; hollow formed, set

Photo by John Carlano

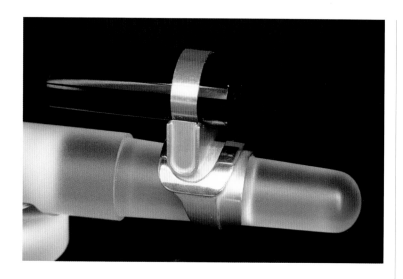

EMILE SOUPLY

Atpat, 1974

4.1 x 2.2 x 4.7 cm

Gold, smoke quartz; hammered, constructed

Photo by artist

KLAUS SPIES

Untitled, 2003

3 x 2.5 x 1 cm

Sterling silver, 18-karat

yellow gold, lapis lazuli

Photo by Larry Sanders

DANIELA HOFFMANN

Buds & Berries: Bouquet Rings, 1999

4 x 2 x 1 cm (each)

Sterling silver, 18-karat yellow gold,

enamel; hand fabricated, torch fired

Photo by George Post

MIWHA OH

Power of Unknown, 1997

2.5 x 3.8 x .6 cm

Steel, 20-karat gold; cast, soldered

Photo by Myung-Wook Huh

(Studio Munch)

MONA TRUNKFIELD

A Ring Not to Do Dishes In, 1973

5 x 4.4 cm

14-karat gold, 18-karat gold,

cloisonné wire, enamel

Photo by artist

STÜCK FINGER UND RING

JI HYE JEON

Rings, 1999

3.2 x 3 x 2.7 cm (left);

3.5 x 3 x .6 cm (right)

Sterling silver; kum-boo

Photo by Myung-Wook Huh

(Studio Munch)

GERD ROTHMANN

Married-Engaged-18th Birthday, 1992

Various dimensions

Silver-plated

Photo by Wilfried Petzi

PIA ALEBORG

Memories, 2003

2.5 x 1.8 x 2.3 cm to

2.5 x 3.3 x 4.7 cm

Brass, silver, enamel

Photo by artist

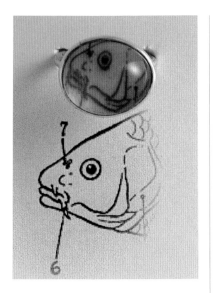

RAMON PUIG CUYÀS

L'esguard, 2002

3 x 2.5 x 1.2 cm

Silver, crystal rock, paper

Photo by artist

SONJA BISCHUR

Spiral Ring, 1992

2.5 x 1 cm

18-karat gold; rolled

Photo by artist

93

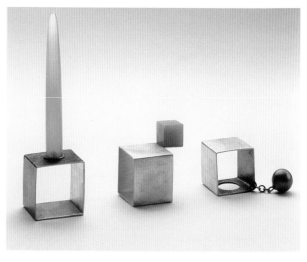

LUDMILA ŠIKOLOVÁ

Three in One: Ring for Architect, 1996

8 x 2.1 x 2.7 cm

Silver, agate, pyrite

Photos by Martin Tůma

MICHAEL CARBERRY

Series of Fine Silver Forged Rings, 2001–2002

3.5 x 3.5 x 1.5 cm (each)

Fine silver; forged

Photo by Joël Degen

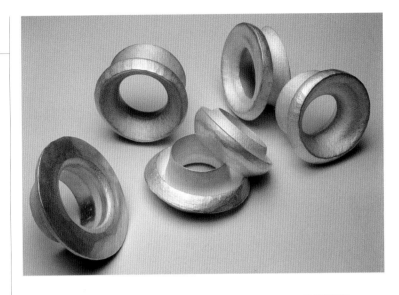

YURI NA

Rings for Filtering II: Flow, 2003

8 x 1.5 x 1.5 cm (each)

Silver, copper, ebony, buffalo
horn; hand constructed

Photo by Myung-Wook Huh
(Studio Munch)

95

SIMMA CHESTER

Millennium Ring with Feet, 2000

5 x 6.9 x 1.3 cm

Sterling silver, fine silver,

freshwater pearls, beads;

fabricated, roller printed

Photo by Hap Sakwa

KENNETH C. MacBAIN

Wedding Rings, 2003

5.7 x 7.6 x 3.8 cm (left);

5.7 x 5.7 x 3.2 cm (right)

Steel, cubic zirconia;

machine cut, soldered

Photo by artist

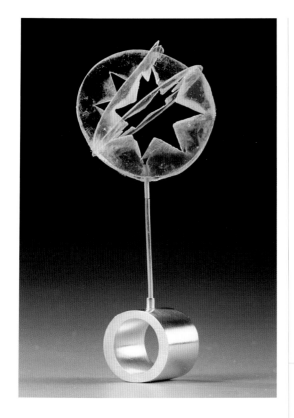

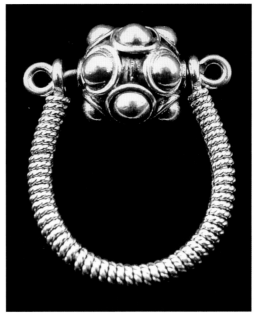

GINA ROTOLO-HARMON

Bumpies!!!, 2003

3.2 x 1.9 x 1.9 cm

Sterling silver bead,

sterling silver wire; wrapped

Photo by artist

SUSAN R. EWING

Prague Star Series: Cosmic Wheel Ring II, 2001

10.2 x 4.4 x 3.8 cm

Sterling silver, mica; hollow constructed

Photo by Jeffrey Sabo

JENNIFER METTLEN NOLAN

Red Twist, 2003

5.7 x 5.1 x 5.1 cm

Glass, silver; lampworked

Photo by Robly A. Glover

LUDMILA ŠIKOLOVÁ

Male and Female Tulip Rings, 2000

10 x 1 x 2.1 cm (left); 15 x .8 x 2.8 cm (right)

Silver, paper, steel, plastic

Photo by Michael Jakoubé

SEUNGHEE OH

Gathering I, II, and III, 2003
3.5 x 4 x 1.2 cm (each)
Silver, amethyst, coral, crystal,
pearl; kum-boo, fabricated
Photos by Kwang-Chun Park
(KC Studio)

CLARA I. ARANA
and GISELLE KOLB
R & M Designs

Rings, 2001
2.2 x 2.2 x 1.6 cm (each)
Sterling silver, acrylic,
Austrian crystal; fabricated
Photo by Peter Groesbeck

SUSAN R. EWING

Prague Star Series: Baroque Ring, 1999

12.7 x 3.8 x 1.6 cm

Sterling silver, found plastic star ornament,
gold leaf, patina; forged, painted, prong set
Collection of the Ohio Craft Museum,
Columbus, Ohio
Photos by Jeffrey Sabo

While living in Prague I became aware of the stars everywhere in my environment, topping more than 150 spires, on the sides of buildings, in windows, and in the street paving. I thought about cosmology, alchemy, the Kabala, Copernicus, and Tycho Brahe, and I adopted these stars in my work.

Susan R. Ewing

TODD REED

Eternity Band Variations, 2003

Various dimensions

Sterling silver, 18-karat yellow gold, cut diamonds,

natural uncut diamond cubes, patina;

forged, fabricated, brushed finish

Photo by Azad

CHRISTEL van der LAAN

Priceless Gems! 1, 2003

7 x 3.5 x 3.5 cm

18-karat gold, polypropylene

swing tags; fabricated

Photo by Robert Frith

101

LORI TALCOTT

Rings, 2002

6.4 x 1.3 cm to 11.4 x 2.5 cm

Silver, brass, 18-karat gold; fabricated

Photo by Douglas Yaple

MARIA CARVALHO

3 in 1, 2003

4.1 x 8.9 x 1.1 cm

Sterling silver wire, fine silver wire,

Biwa pearl; fabricated

Photo by Sergio Henrique V. Alberti

RACHIK SOUSSI

Bague Armure (Armor Ring), 2002

2.5 x 2.5 x 1.3 cm

Silver; hand fabricated

Photo by artist

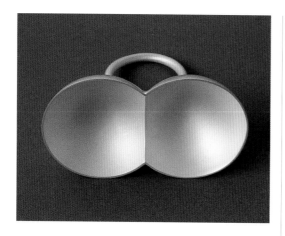

THERESE HILBERT

Untitled, 2003

3.5 x 5.3 x 3.1 cm

Sterling silver

Photo by Otto Künzli

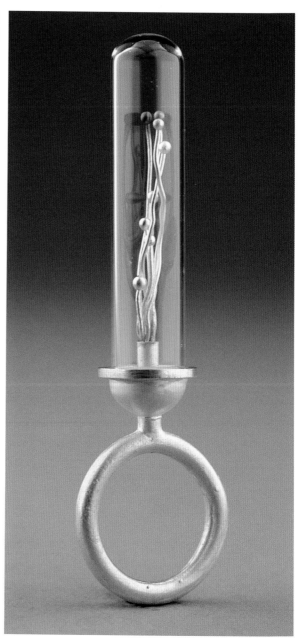

MORIKI TOMIHARA

Test Tube Ring, 2003

7.6 x 2.5 x 1.3 cm

Fine silver, sterling silver, 24-karat

gold plate; cast, fabricated

Photo by Donovan Widmer

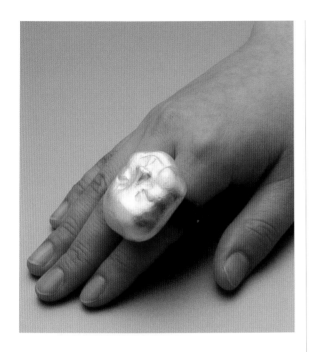

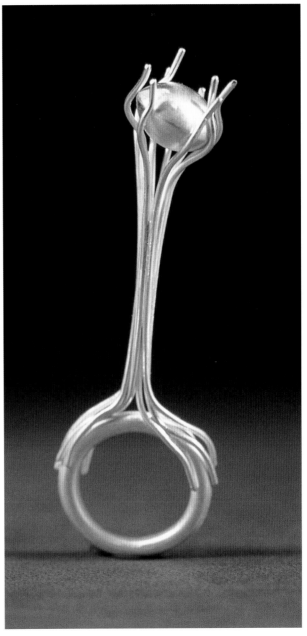

SO-YOUNG KIM

Trace of Image, 2003

3.3 x 3.8 x 4.5 cm

Silver, buffalo horn

Photo by Myung-Wook Huh

(Studio Munch)

SUSAN J. SKOCZEN

Bud, 2001

7.6 x 3.2 x 1.9 cm

Sterling silver; fabricated

Photo by artist

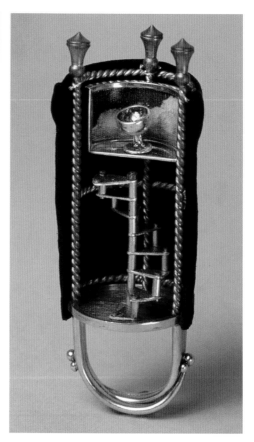

KELLY HUNTER

Surprise, 2002

6.4 x 6.4 x 6.4 cm

Sterling silver, patina, synthetic

stones, glass, resin; hollow

constructed, hinged, cast, textured

Photos by Taweesak Molsawat

KIRSTEN ROOK

The Big Quest-ion, 1996

7.6 x 2.5 x 2.5 cm

Sterling silver, fabric, photocopied

image; fabricated, sewn

Photo by Bobby Hanson

SERGEY BOGDANOV

Untitled, 2003

4.4 x 3.5 cm

18-karat white gold, grey

agate, synthetic ruby

Photo by Joël Degen

MARK NUELL

Untitled, 2003

3.5 x 3 x 2.7 cm

Silver, pink tourmaline, 22-karat

gold; hand forged, coiled, set

Photo by Peter White

SUSAN ZEISS
Ring, 2000
2.8 x 2.4 x 1.9 cm
14-karat gold, pearl;
mitsuro-hikime wax
technique, lost wax cast
Photo by Douglas Yaple

● **Mitsu (honey) ro (wax) hiki (drawing) me (texture).** The past several years, I have researched and formulated a wax, *mitsuro hikime*, which, during processing, develops a unique linear pattern. This technique is very recognizable and appealing. Mitsuro hikime will bend and curl, giving surface detail and a wonderful fluid quality. Along with these interesting properties come some technical challenges. When warm enough to work, the wax will slump. When cool enough to hold shape, it is very brittle and will crack with the slightest shock.

Susan Zeiss

JANIS KERMAN

Rings, 2002

1.9 x 1.9 cm (left); 1.9 x 2.5 cm (right)

18-karat white gold, 18-karat yellow gold,

mabe pearl, umba sapphire (left);

18-karat gold, Tahitian mabe pearl,

umba sapphires (right)

Photo by Larry Turner

NOEL ARONOV

Swoop Ring, 1995

2.5 x 1.3 cm

18-karat gold, platinum, diamond, pearl;

fabricated, anticlastic raising

Photo by Vermillion Photographic

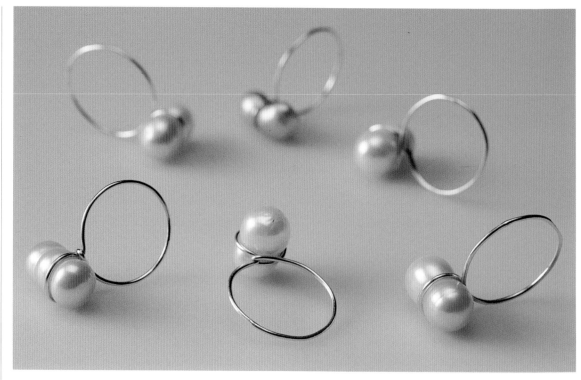

SILKE SPITZER

Paps (Papillions), 2003

Various dimensions

Sterling silver, pearls

Photo by Petra Jaschke

OWEN MAPP

Pacific Memories, 2003

5.5 x 4 cm

Bone; hand carved

Photo by artist

VANESSA SAMUELS

Layers #2, 2003

2 x 2.5 x .5 cm

Beef bone, sterling silver;

carved, constructed, fabricated

Photo by artist

KAYO SAITO

Swaying Rings, 2001

15 x 6 x 6 cm (each)

Japanese handmade paper, silver, stainless

steel wire; coiled, covered, coated

Photo by artist

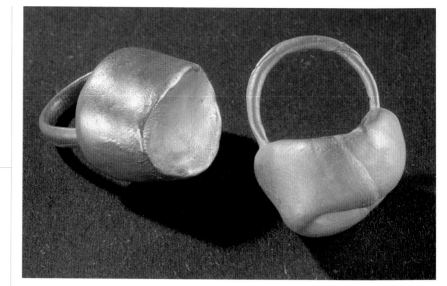

JOHANNA DAHM

Ashante, 1998

3.3 x 2.5 x 1.5 cm (each)

18-karat yellow gold;

lost wax cast

Photo by Reinhard Zimmermann

ASA HALLDIN

Rings of Bronze, 2003

3 x 2 x 1.5 cm (left);

3 x 3 x 2 cm (right)

Bronze; lost wax cast

Photo by Adrian Nordenborg

JAEHYUNG CHO

A Peanut in My Memory, 2003
3.5 x 4 x 2 cm
Sterling silver, gold leaf; kum-boo
Photos by Myung-Wook Huh
(Studio Munch)

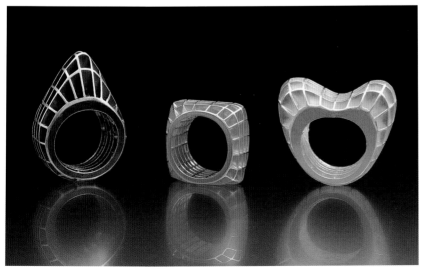

ANYA PINCHUK

Grid Rings, 2002
3.2 x 2.5 x 1.9 cm (average)
Sterling silver, 18-karat gold;
fabricated
Photo by artist

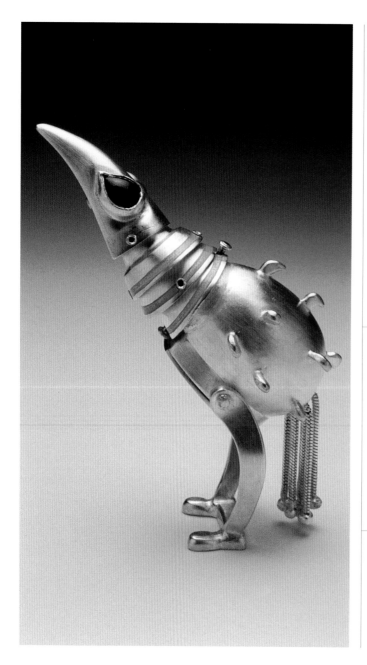

KIRK LANG

Mars, 2003

5 x 2.5 x 1.3 cm

Stainless steel, 14-karat yellow

gold, meteorite, coral

Photo by artist

RIE TANIGUCHI

Helmut II Ring/Box, 2001

3.5 x 2.2 x 6 cm

Sterling silver, amethyst, enamel,

stainless steel spring; press

formed, soldered, riveted, pegged

Photo by Joël Degen

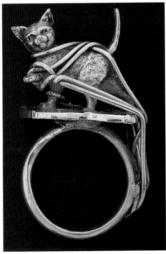

COLIN McDONALD

Cock Ring, 2001

20.3 x 5 x 5 cm

Sterling silver, freshwater pearl;

soldered, fabricated

Photo by artist

ROBERT COOGAN

Bondage Series, 2000–2003

4.4 x 2.5 x .9 cm

Sterling silver; cast

Photos by TTU Photo Services

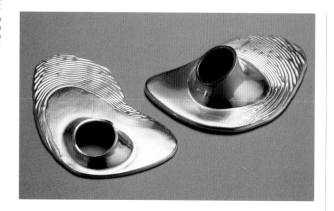

SUNGHO CHO

Soak My Finger (In the Sea), 2003

8 x 4.5 x 1.5 cm (left); 8 x 5.5 x 2 cm (right)

Sterling silver; cast

Photo by Myung-Wook Huh (Studio Munch)

● As the ring is worn, the fine crochet work becomes frayed and disintegrates, leaving the silver rings behind. This symbolizes the period of mourning after the death of a dear one. The silver rings stay on as a memory.

Miriam Verbeek

MIRIAM VERBEEK

Rouwring (Mourning Ring), 1993

10 x 15 x 2.5 cm

Silver, silk, net; crocheted

Photo by Hennie van Beek

KATJA KORSAWE

Two for Ten, 2002

2 x 2 x 5 cm (each)

Silver, leather

Courtesy of Galerie V & V, Vienna, Austria

Photo by artist

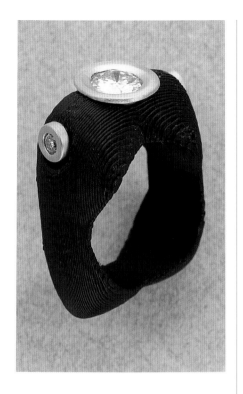

SUE ANN DORMAN

Cad/Cam Ring, 2003

3.2 x 2.5 x .9 cm

22-karat gold, moissanite, diamonds,
metal rod; computer designed,
machine molded, cast, set

Photo by Steve Alfano

FRIEDRICH MÜLLER

Ringspiel (Ring Play), 1995

2.6 x 2 x .8 cm

Inox steel, hard plastic
(Ertacetal® Pom); turned

Photo by Thomas Wiedmer

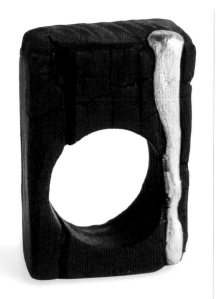

ALESSIA SEMERARO

Untitled, 2002

4 x 2.5 x 1.5 cm

Cedar wood, metal, resin;

constructed, poured, burnt, coated

Photo by Fabio Valenti

● I live in a beautiful, rural part of Sonoma County, California. My husband found a handful of square rusty nails when he was repairing the sheep fence. This ring was first inspired by my desire to use the nail, but also by the lovely mossy green on the wood, the old wire lashing pickets together, and the way that nature was reclaiming human efforts and materials.

Ellen Cheek

ELLEN CHEEK

The Old Sheep Fence, 2000

2.5 x 2.2 x .9 cm

Fine silver, sterling silver, copper, gesso, colored pencil, rusted antique steel nail; fabricated

Photo by Hap Sakwa

SUSAN J. SKOCZEN

3 Wood Rings, 1998

6.4 x 2.5 x 2.5 cm (largest)

Sterling silver, copper, padouk,

cherry, poplar; fabricated

Photo by artist

LIZ SCHOCK

Tomatillo Rings, 2002

9.5 x 8.9 x 1.9 cm (left);

8.9 x 6.4 x 2.5 cm (right)

Tomatillo wrappers,

copper thread; sewn

Photo by Dean Spencer

ANTJE FREIHEIT

Ring for Two Fingers, 2001

2.7 x 4 x 1.8 cm

Sterling silver, 18-karat gold,

melaphyre; constructed

Photo by Ursula Dannien

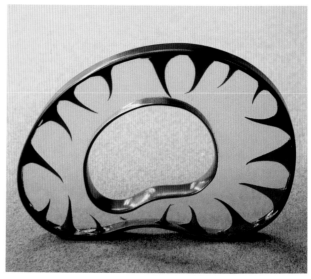

DANIELA MLÁDENKOVÁ

Jewelry for Touch, 1998

5.8 x 4 x .6 cm

Copper, rose thorns,

polyester resin; cast

Photo by artist

THIERRY BONTRIDDER

5 Rings in Box, 1999

Various dimensions

Boxwood; milled, lathe worked

Photo by Paul Louis

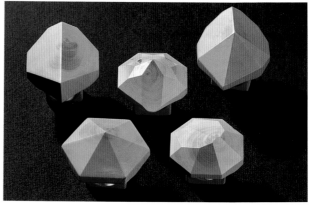

BETTINA DITTLMANN and MICHAEL JANK

Foreverrings, 2001–2003

5 x 2.2 x 2 cm to 3.5 x 4 x 3 cm

Copper, fine silver, fine gold, iron; center punched, forged

Photo by artists

TOGETHER
Gold
Silver
Copper
Forging
Growing
Piece
By
Piece
Everything that happens is important
Center yourself, he said
Bettina Dittlmann and Michael Jank

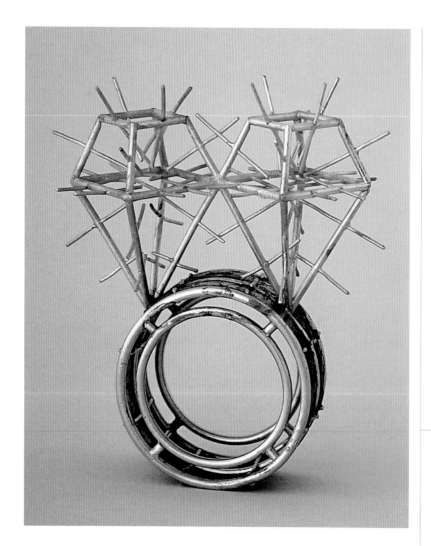

PHILIP SAJET

Cactus Ring Double, 2003

4.5 x 3.5 x 2 cm

Gold, iron rust

Photo by artist

MIE HORIUCHI

Noodle Rings, 2003
8.9 x 2.5 x 10.2 cm (each)
Sterling silver, somen
noodles; wax cast
Photo by Mary Bausman

SEUNG JIN LEE

Accumulated Form, 2002
Various dimensions
Mokume gane, wood, fish
fossil, dinosaur bone fossil
Photo by Myung-Wook Huh
(Studio Munch)

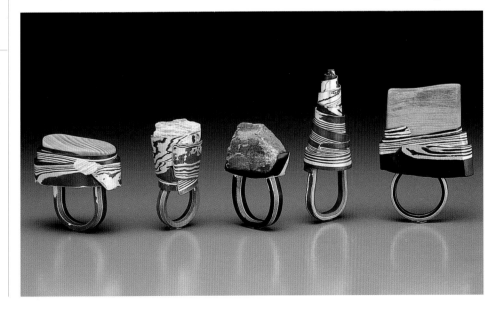

123

CATHERINE S. M. CHUI

Cherish Nature, 2001

4.4 x 2.5 x 3 cm

Aluminum, pumice stone

Photo by William M. F. Lui

PETER HOOGEBOOM

Lotus Rings, 1996

3.7 x 2.7 x 1.5 cm (left); 4.6 x 2.6 x 1.5 cm (right)

Silver, gold, glazed ceramics

Photo by Henni van Beek

PAVEL HERYNEK

Ring for the Finger, 2001

4.5 x 5.1 x 3.4 cm

Cork, silver

Courtesy of Galerie V & V, Vienna, Austria

Photo by Markéta Ondrusková

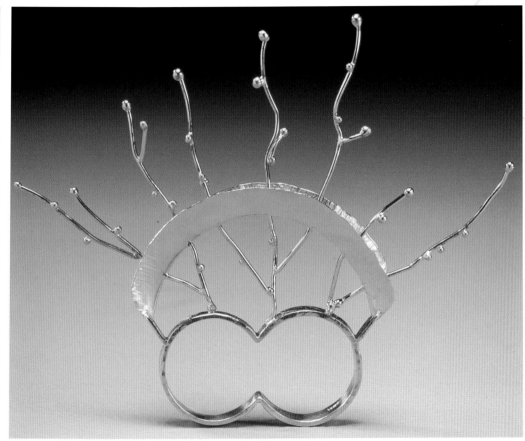

YOSHIKO YAMAMOTO

Umegaka (Two-Finger Ring), 2000

7.6 x 9.5 x .6 cm

18-karat yellow gold, 18-karat

white gold; fabricated

Courtesy of Mobilia Gallery,

Cambridge, Massachusetts

Photo by Dean Powell

A piece of jewelry is, above all, a concept, an idea. If on the one hand such a concept has to be subordinated to the material, it is, on the other hand, also deeply inspired by it. Through the connection of precious metals, stones, and unconventional materials, I create unique objects, which make the extraordinary wearable. This has been the stimulus and demand of my creative work.

Michael Zobel

MICHAEL ZOBEL

Ring, 2002

2.6 cm

18-karat gold, platinum,

Context Cut® light

yellow diamond

Photo by Fred Thomas

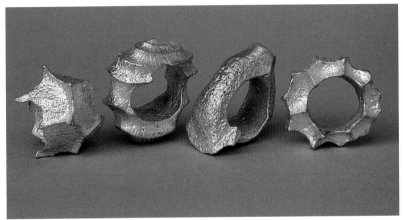

JOHANNA DAHM

Anti-Ashanti, 2002

3 x 2 cm

Fine silver; cast

Photo by artist

KYOKO URINO

Untitled, 2000

2 x 1.5 x 2 cm

Silver-plated wire, gold-plated wire,

oxidized wire; crocheted, constructed

Photo by Kuniyasu Usui

KELLY HUNTER

Spiral, 2002

5 x 5 x 5 cm

Sterling silver, sapphire;

wax carved, cast

Photo by Taweesak Molsawat

127

WILLIAM SCHOLL

Untitled, 2001

2.5 x 2.5 x 1.9 cm

18-karat yellow gold, yellow chrysoberyl, tourmalines,

yellow sapphire, blue sapphire; fabricated

Photo by Ralph Gabriner

ANJA SCHÖNMEYER

Ring, 1997

2.7 x 2.7 x .7 cm

18-karat gold; rolled

Photo by Beate Leonards

VAUNE MASON

Cathedral, 2003

7.9 x 2.3 x 2.2 cm

Sterling silver; fabricated,

cast, oxidized

Photo by Julian Tyerman

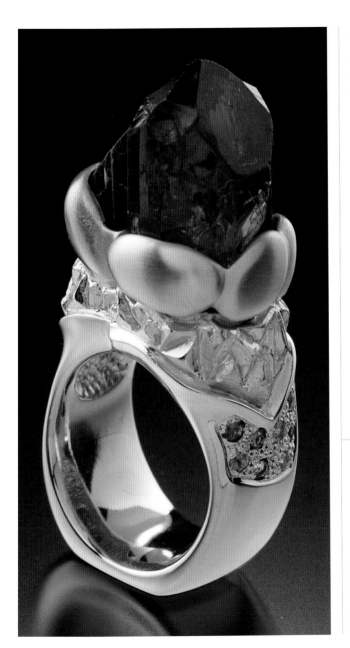

This ring is a tribute to tanzanite and its country of origin, Tanzania. It recognizes the hardships of those mining this most extraordinary gem.

John Strobel

JOHN STROBEL

Kilimanjaro, 2002

4.4 x 3.2 x 2.5 cm

18-karat green gold, platinum,

tanzanite crystal, Paraíba tourmaline,

tsavorite garnets; cast, set

Photo by Larry Sanders

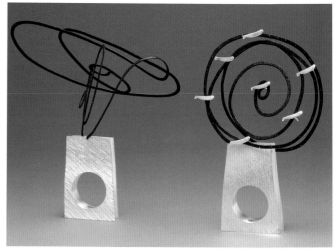

SUNGHO CHO

A Monument for the Sea, 2002

9 x 6.5 x 10 cm (left); 6 x 2.5 x 9.5 cm (right)

Sterling silver, iron

Photos by Myung-Wook Huh (Studio Munch)

OWEN MAPP

Ancestral Memories, 2003

10 x 4 cm

Bone; hand carved

Photo by artist

HANNE ERIKSEN MAPP

Wave Finder, 2003

6 x 4.5 cm

Mammoth ivory, sterling silver; fabricated

Photo by artist

CHRISTEL VAN DER LAAN

Priceless Gems! 2, 2003

6.5 x 4 x 1.5 cm

18-karat gold, polypropylene

swing tags; fabricated

Photo by Robert Frith

MARIANNA WOMBLE

In-decision, 2003

3.5 x 3.5 cm

Sterling silver, epoxy resin,

ball bearings, stainless steel;

fabricated, inlaid

Photo by Larry Sanders

We live in our own baskets, each with balls of yarn, a paddle, and a rudder; afloat in a world of unfathomable depths. To amuse ourselves, we sing and fill our baskets with beautiful things, art. To keep from being lonely we throw out threads to other baskets and tie our floating worlds together. Art sings to our soul, gives us meaning, and connects us to others. It's our life thread.

Marianna Womble

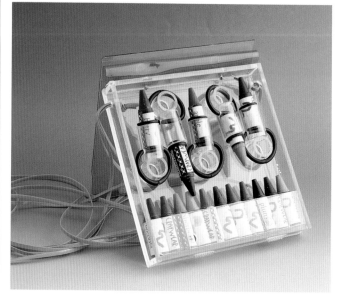

LAURA ARAGON

Sweet Sixteen, 2002

1.3 x 10.2 x 10.2 cm

Plexiglas®, clear tubing,

crayons, O-rings

Photo by Rachelle Thiewes

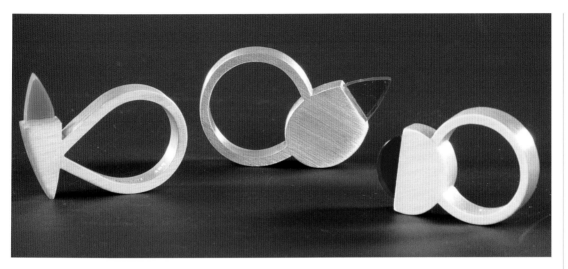

LISA VERSHBOW

Neon Trio, 2003

3.2 x 1.9 x .6 cm (each)

Sterling silver, Plexiglas®; fabricated

Photo by Boris Bendikov

JAN MATTHESIUS

My Inner Self, 2002

3 x 6 x 3 cm

Gold, topaz, fire opal

Photo by Rob Glastra

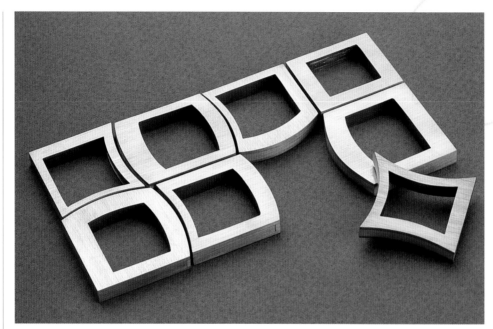

PETRINA KERNCHEN

Puzzle Rings, 2001

2.5 x 2.5 x 4 cm

Stainless steel, 9-karat gold; laser cut,
spot welded, inlaid

Photo by Kevin Killey

⬤ By chance, a new
material suddenly
appeared—Corian®!
These rings are prod-
ucts of my imagination
and come out sponta-
neously. There are
neither drawings nor
concepts, and they are
produced in the think-
ing of an eye, in other
words, during the work.
Every decision comes
about according to an
inner emotion at the
moment concerned.

Fritz Maierhofer

FRITZ MAIERHOFER

Ring I, 2001

7 x 4 x 1.3 cm

Corian®, platinum

Photo by artist

MONICA CECCHI

Senza Conservanti, 2002

3.6 x 2.4 x 2 cm

Iron, gold, tin can; constructed

Photo by Federico Cavicchioli

FLORIAN LADSTAETTER

Reaktorring, 1991

30 x 14 x 10 cm

Silver, balsa wood, gold plate; cast

Photo by artist

SUSAN KASSON SLOAN

Confetti Rings, 2003

3.2 x 3.2 x 2.5 cm (each)

Sterling silver, 18-karat gold,

epoxy resin, pigments

Photo by Ralph Gabriner

ROY

Pittsburgh Rings, 2003

4.4 x 3.8 x 2.6 cm (largest)

Silver; fabricated

Photo by Dean Powell

SHONA RAE

The Three Spinners, 2002

27.9 x 6.4 x 5 cm

Sterling silver, bronze,

router bearing; cast

Photo by artist

AI MORITA

Kinetic Puzzle Ring, 2003

1.2 x 3 x 3 cm

18-karat gold, peridot, blue topaz

Photo by artist

ULO FLORACK

Every Tube Has Its Secret, 1999

5 x 4 x 2 cm

Silver, gold plate, enamel;

lost wax cast

Photo by artist

YVONNE KURZ

The Ring Thing, 2001
2 x 2 x 1.2 cm (each)
Rubber, glass, plastic
Photo by Petra Jaschke

KAZ ROBERTSON

Wobble Rings, 2001
7 x 2.5 x 1.2 cm (largest)
Silver, magnets, resin
Photo by John K. McGregor

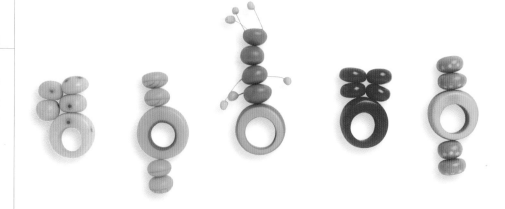

138

KATY HACKNEY

Wobbly Pronged Ring, 1999

5 x 4 x 3 cm (kinetic element)

Cellulose acetate, silver; laminated,
hand carved, cast

Photo by Joël Degan

CHELSEA STONE

Carnival Rings, 2001

1.3 x 2.5 x 2.5 cm to 5 x 2.5 x 2.5 cm

Silver, enamel, gemstones, lampworked glass

Photo by Robly A. Glover

SUSANNE KLEMM

red single & massive attack, 2001

4 x 2 x 1 cm (each)

Silver, varnish; soldered

Courtesy of Galerie Ra,
Amsterdam, Netherlands

Photo by artist

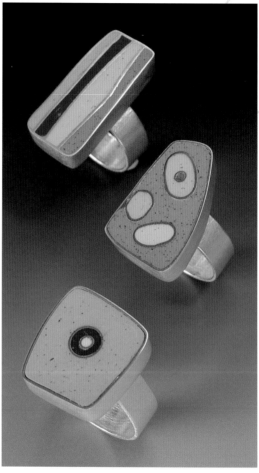

Our work speaks of the same patterns in nature that are found from the cellular to the celestial.

Lou Ann Townsend and Mary V. Filapek

JOSÉE DESJARDINS

How Can You Release This Torrent?, 1999

5.3 x 2.8 x 2.8 cm

Sterling silver, enamel, vermeil, pebbles,

carnelian, siliconized tile grout;

lost wax cast, mosaic

Photo by Paul Simon

LOU ANN TOWNSEND and MARY V. FILAPEK

Cellular Trio, 2003

2.6 x 2.1 x 3.2 cm (top); 2.6 x 2.1 x 2.7 cm

(center); 2.6 x 2.1 x 1.9 cm (bottom)

Silver, polymer clay; constructed, inlaid

Photo by Margot Geist

JU-NAM KIM

System Ring Series, 2000

Various dimensions

Sterling silver, gold, sodalite

Photos by artist

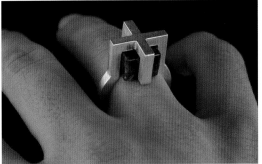

TOM FERRERO

Queen Elizabeth Ring, 2002
2.5 x 3.8 x 3.8 cm
Sterling silver, 22-karat gold;
fabricated, stamped
Photo by Dan Neuburger

LORI WARREN

5 Golden Rings, 2003
Various dimensions
14-karat yellow gold, diamonds,
steel; fabricated, cast
Photo by artist

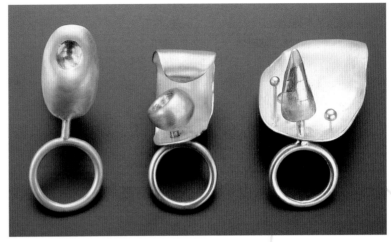

NAOMI TACHIBANA

My Garden, 2003

3.9 x 2.8 x 1.5 cm

Silver, diamonds

Photo by Federico Cavicchioli

❦ I enjoy constructing pieces that contain some element of surprise that cannot immediately be seen by the observer, such as a textured design on the inside of a ring or a moving part on top.

Naomi Tachibana

KAORI WATANABE

Seed of Love, 2003

5.2 x 2.1 x 1 cm (left); 4.2 x 2.1 x 2 cm (center); 4.7 x 3.2 x 4.2 cm (right)

Silver, 24-karat gold; embossed, hammered, kum-boo

Photo by Federico Cavicchioli

❦ I found that we all have a "seed of love" inside of us. I just want to make it grow.

Kaori Watanabe

ÚRSULA VIÑOLAS SUBIRANA

Expectation, 2003

9 x 5 x 4 cm

Silver, sea urchin, turquoise; hand

fabricated, lost wax cast

Photo by Josep Vallès Reixach

ANANDA KHALSA

Bamboo Ring, 2003

2.5 x 1.9 x 1.6 cm

Acrylic paint, paper,

sterling silver, glass

Photo by Azad

YVONNE KURZ

Mantel Rings, 2001–2003

5 cm high (each)

Felt, glass, cotton, silver,

steel cable; sewn

Photo by artist

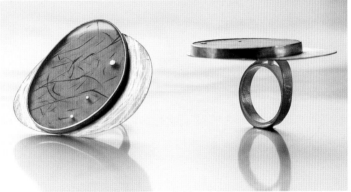

MARZIA ROSSI

Untitled, 2003

2.8 x 4 x 3 cm (each)

Plexiglas®, silver, red paint

Photo by Federico Cavicchioli

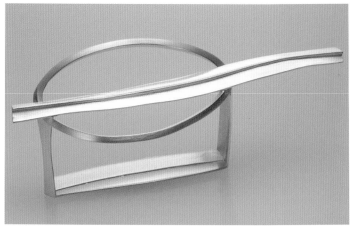

EUNJOO PARK

Linear Ring, 2003

3.8 x 3 x 2 cm

Sterling silver

Photo by Kwang-Chun Park (KC Studio)

BARBARA COHEN

Cocooned, 2003

4.4 x 3.8 x 1.9 cm

Sterling silver, silk cocoon,

paint; cast, fabricated

Photo by artist

CHRIS TINNEN

Abstraction Kit (Incisor, Retractor,
Extractor), 2003

8 x 3 x 1 cm (left); 6 x 5 x 2 cm

(center); 4 x 10 x 1 cm (right)

Stainless steel; fabricated

Photo by artist

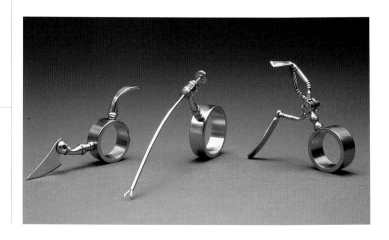

ROBERT COOGAN

Blade Ring, 2002

7.6 x 2.5 x .5 cm

Damascus steel, mokume gane,

sterling silver; forged, fabricated

Photo by TTU Photo Services

TAKAKO MURAMATSU

Globe, 2002

3.8 x 2.5 x 2.5 cm

Sterling silver, rock; soldered,

drilled, cold connected

Photo by Sylvia Montana

ADAM PAXON

Squirming Ring with Tail, 2002
5 x 3.1 x 3.1 cm
Transparent, fluorescent, and
mirrored acrylic, silver leaf;
laminated, carved, polished
Photo by Graham Lees

JANET TEOH

Reaching, Stretching...etc., 2000
12 x 3.5 x 2 cm
Paper, acrylic paint, fishing line
Photo by artist

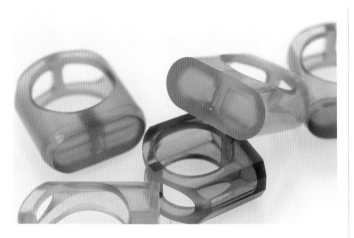

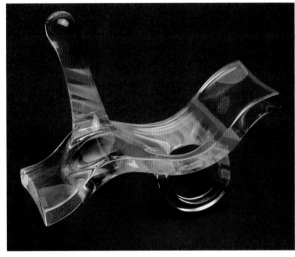

MIKIKO MINEWAKI

Lighters, 2002

2.8 x 2.5 x .8 cm

Disposable lighters; cut, filed

Photo by artist

WIM van DOORSCHODT

Water, 2001

9.5 x 6 x 5 cm

Acrylic; laminated, cut, filed,

drilled, lathe sculpted

Photo by Tom Noz

DANA ROTH

Beer Can Rings, 2002

1 cm wide (each)

Sterling silver, aluminum

beverage cans

Photo by artist

JEANNE BEAVER

*The Space That Tension
Occupies*, 1998
5 x 33 x 1.3 cm
Sterling silver, stainless steel;
cold connected, soldered,
hollow constructed
Photos by artist

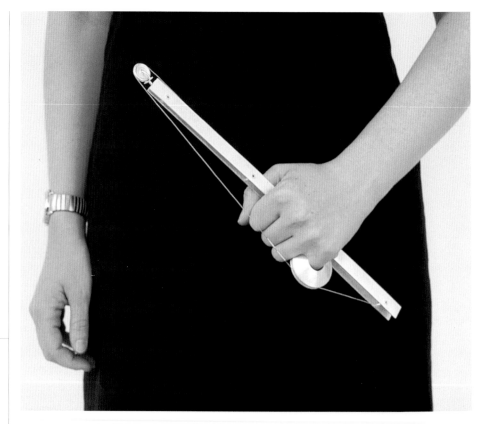

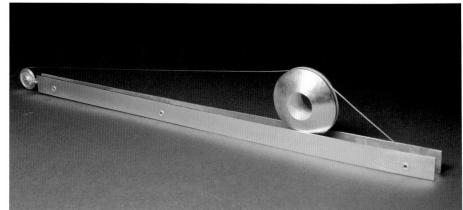

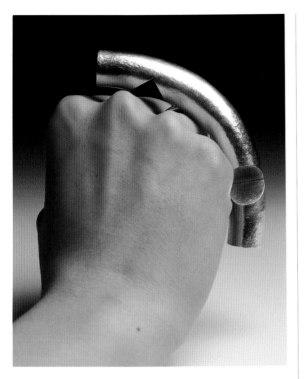

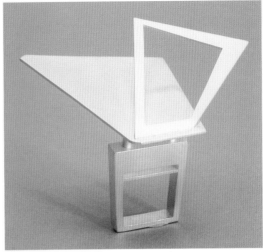

MIZUKO YAMADA

Silver Ring, 2003

3.5 x 10 x 1.5 cm

Silver; hammered, soldered

Photo by Toshihide Kajihara

ADDAM

Fliight, 2002

5 x 7.3 x 6.4 cm

Sterling silver, sheet metal;

cast, fabricated, soldered

Photos by Victor France & Alan Webster

MARK HARDIN

Gold Ring, 1990

2.5 x 2.5 x .6 cm

18-karat to 20-karat yellow

gold nuggets; soldered

Photo by artist

SUSAN WISE and JEFF WISE

Carousel, 1999

3.8 x 2.5 x 2.5 cm

18-karat gold, sugilite, garnet;

fabricated, carved

Photo by artists

WESLEY GLEBE

Finger Rings, 2003

Various dimensions

Titanium, 24-karat gold, stainless

steel, platinum; cold connected

Photo by Michael Black

PEG FETTER

Street Cleaner, 2002

2.2 x 2.2 x 1.3 cm

Found iron street-cleaning bristles,

14-karat yellow gold; fabricated, forged

Photo by Don Casper

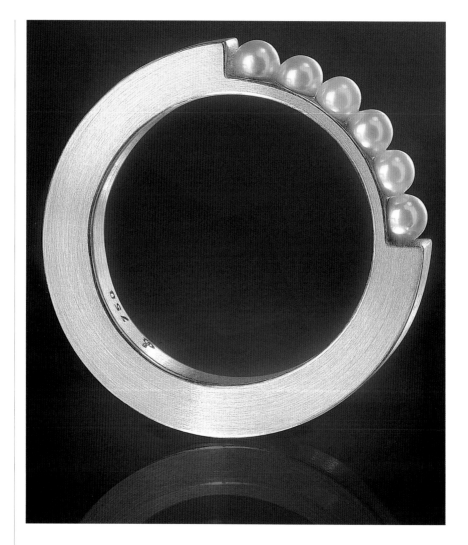

ANDREA BRACHTHÄUSER

Quarter, 2002

.3 cm deep

18-karat yellow gold, Akoya cultured pearls

Photo by Marc Strunz (Spotlight Photo Studio)

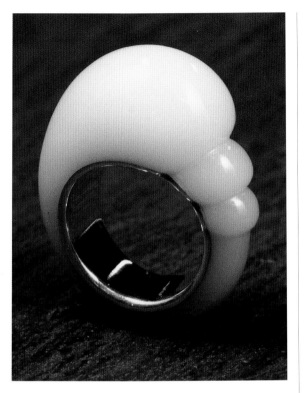

FRANK MOLNAR

Ring Carved Stone, 1997

4.1 x 1.3 x 2.5 cm

Blue chalcedony, silver

Photo by artist

JACK and ELIZABETH GUALTIERI
ZAFFIRO GOLDSMITHING

Lotus Ring, 2001

2.5 x 2.5 x 3.5 cm

22-karat yellow gold, 18-karat yellow gold,
green tourmaline, labradorite; hand
fabricated, torch-fusion granulated

Photo by Daniel Van Rossen

JOE REYES APODACA

Cosmic Connection, 2002

2.4 x 1.9 x 1.9 cm

14-karat gold, meteorite,
Australian opal, diamond brilliant;
fabricated, die formed, cut,
etched, inlaid
Photo by Hap Sakwa

MICHELLE GRIFFITH PERLICH

Crude, 2002

2.5 x 1.3 x .6 cm

18-karat gold, sterling silver;
fabricated, hollow form constructed
Photo by Hap Sakwa

HELFRIED KODRÉ

Amy, 1999

3.5 x 4.2 x 1.3 cm

Gold, white gold; soldered

Photo by artist

ALAN ARDIFF

Element of Surprise, 2003

2 x 2 x .8 cm

18-karat yellow gold,

18-karat white gold, topaz

Photos by Michael Blake

157

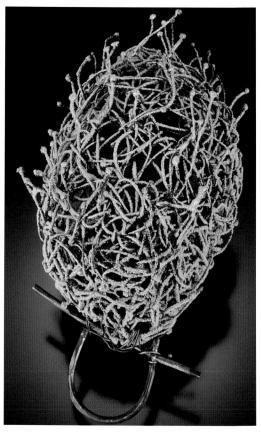

SERGEY JIVETIN

Wad-o-Greenbacks Ring, 2003

4.4 x 3.2 x 1.3 cm

18-karat green gold; rolled, riveted

Photo by artist

RUTHANN GRAZIER

#27, from the *Metamorphosis Series*, 2003

10.8 x 5 x 5 cm

Copper wire, opaque enamel;

tension fabricated

Photo by Robert Diamante

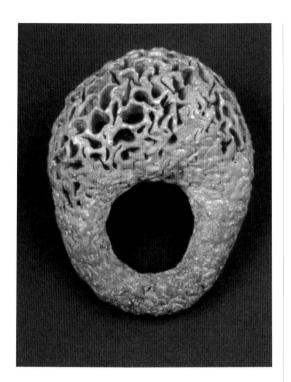

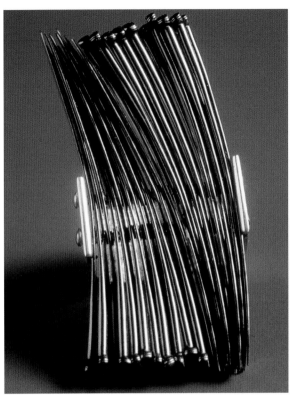

INA SEIDL

Untitled, 2001

5.2 x 4.2 x 3 cm

Silver; lost wax cast

Photo by artist

TONE VIGELAND

Ring II, 1982

4.1 x 2 x 1.8 cm

Steel, 18-karat gold, silver, forged steel nails

Photo by Guri Dahl

FRITZ MAIERHOFER

Ring III, 2002

5 x 3.5 x 1.3 cm

Corian®, yellow gold

Photo by artist

MARGIT HART

Rings, 2002

6.3 x 2.2 x .5 cm (top); 4.1 x 2.7 x .7 cm (bottom)

Silver, bronze; modeled, cast

Photo by artist

KAREN McCREARY

Terrazzo Rings, 1997

3.2 x 2.5 x .6 cm (each)

Sterling silver, acrylic,

resin; fabricated, cast

Photo by artist

TERI BLOND

Bug Ring, 2003

5.7 x 3.8 x 2.8 cm

Sterling silver, pearls, amethyst, red coral, emerald,

faux ruby, black permanent marker, silver paint,

blue-violet glitter, epoxy resin; hand fabricated

Photos by Harry Geyer

161

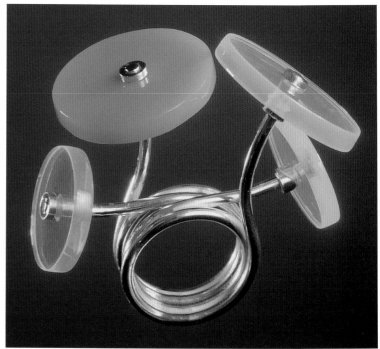

CYNTHIA TOOPS

Wheat Grass, 2003

5 x 2.2 x 1 cm

Polymer clay

Photo by Roger Schreiber

ANNETTE TJHO

Say Cheese, 2003

5 x 4.5 x 2.5 cm

Silver, Plexiglas®; riveted, polished

Photo by Hans Breuer

ROSIE DONOVAN

Displacement #1, 2001

3.1 x 2.7 x 1.7 cm

Jade, reticulated silver, sterling silver,

epoxy resin; carved, sandblasted

Photo by Jon Walker

WIM van DOORSCHODT

Water, 2001

9.5 x 5 x 5 cm

Acrylic; laminated, carved, filed,

drilled, lathe sculpted

Photo by Tom Noz

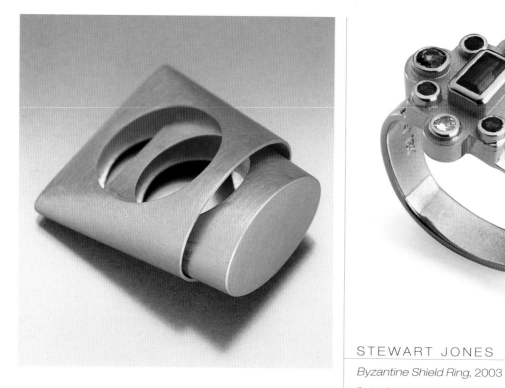

STEWART JONES

Byzantine Shield Ring, 2003

2.4 x 2.1 x 1.9 cm

18-karat yellow gold, orange sapphire,

green tourmalines, diamonds, rubies;

hand fabricated

Photo by Tim Hall

ETSUKO SONOBE

Untitled, 2002

2.6 x 3 x 1.5 cm

20-karat gold

Photo by Okinari Kurokawa

JAN MATTHESIUS

Wilhelmina Ring, 2002

2 x 2.5 x 2 cm (base for

interchangeable elements)

Titanium, gold, diamond, magnet

Photo by Ger van Leeuwen

BEATE KLOCKMANN

Big Amber Ring, 2002

7 x 4.5 x 3 cm

Amber, 18-karat gold; hammered,

milled, folded, soldered

Photo by artist

CHRISTOPHER C. DARWAY

Notch Ring, from the *Self-Adjustable Series*, 2002

2.5 x .6 x 1.9 cm

14-karat gold, stainless steel wire,

hematite bead; cast, sandblasted

Photo by Chet Bolins

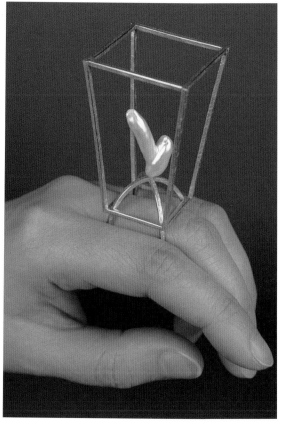

LIAUNG-CHUNG YEN

A Space or a Cage for Myself, 2003

7.9 x 3.5 x 3.5 cm

14-karat gold, pearl; fabricated

Photo by Dan Neuberger

ROBIN MARTIN-CUST

Untitled, 1998

1.9 x 1.9 x 1.3 cm

Found pitted steel, 18-karat gold,

nickel; fabricated

Photo by Ken Woisard

CHRISTIAN SONNLEITNER

Philipp Says More Light III, 2002

3.5 x 2.5 x 1.7 cm

Silver, rock crystal

Courtesy of Galerie V & V, Vienna, Austria

Photo by artist

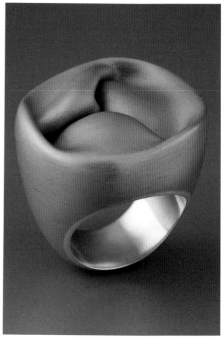

KATHRYN OSGOOD

Remember Me, 2003

7.6 x 2.5 x 2.5 cm

Sterling silver, enamel,

copper; fabricated

Photo by Robert Diamante

YUYEN CHANG

Ring, from the *Orifice Series*, 2003

2.5 x 2.5 x 3.2 cm

Copper, sterling silver

Photo by Jamie Young

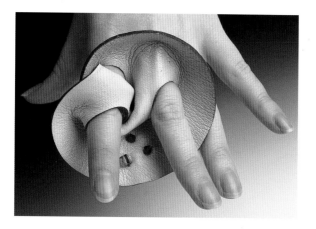

MELISSA DUGGAN

Twist Ring, 2002

10.2 cm in diameter (flat)

Leather, crystal beads,

acrylic paint

Photo by Tom Van Enyde

LINDA THREADGILL

Group of Garden Rings, 1999

Various dimensions

Sterling silver; constructed, etched

Photo by James Threadgill

LYNDA ANDREWS-BARRY

Cone Flower Ring, 2002

6.5 x 3.2 x 3.8 cm

Echinacea (purple cone flower) seed head,

tulip poplar stamen, sterling silver, patina;

fabricated, electroformed, cast

Photo by Ralph Gabriner

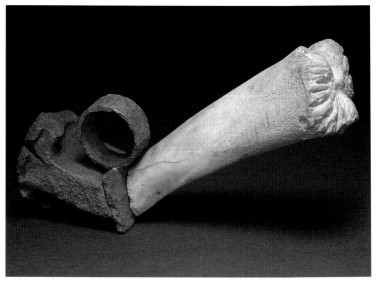

CHRISTOPH ZELLWEGER

Ring, 1992

7 x 15 x 5 cm

Found bone, found iron tool

Collection of Angermuseum, Erfurt, Germany

Photo by artist

DAN SAEGER

Burying the Hatchet Ring, 2003

8.9 x 3.8 x 3.8 cm

Sterling silver, hedge wood, stainless steel

Photo by artist

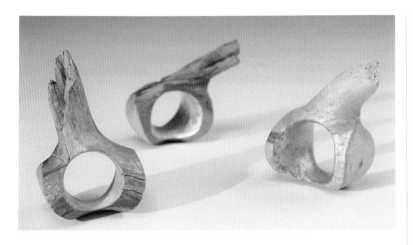

LUZIA VOGT

Lost and Found, 2002

5 x 3 x 2 cm (each)

Found wood, gold foil, silver foil

Photo by artist

ADAM CLARK

Jeopardy, 2003

3.8 x 3.8 x 3.8 cm

Sterling silver, glass eye, carnelian

Photo by Hap Sakwa

THOMAS MANN

Stone Fetish Rings, 2003

Various dimensions

Silver, iron, bronze, beach
rocks; fabricated

Photo by Angele Seiley

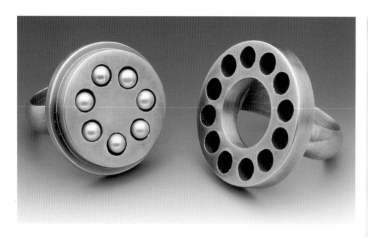

ELISA BONGFELDT

2 Rings, 2002

3.2 x 2.5 x 2.5 cm

Sterling silver, freshwater pearls; fabricated

Photo by George Post

BELINDA HAGER

Southern Cross, 2002

1.5 x 2.1 x 2.1 cm

Niobium, diamonds

Photo by artist

HANNE BEHRENS

Ring, 2001

4 x 3 x 2 cm

Silver, 18-karat gold; braided, hollow form constructed, soldered, oxidized

Photo by artist

HWA-JIN KIM

Recollection Running, 2003
2.5 x 1.8 x .7 cm to
3 x 3.3 x 1.8 cm
Sterling silver; cast
Photos by In-Soo Lee

LAURA LAPACHIN

Finger Bag Rings, 2000
Various dimensions
Linoleum, silver, thread;
fabricated, heat fused
Photo by artist

173

BIC TIEU

Integrated Box Ring Series, 2003

2.7 x 2.7 x 2.5 cm (each)

18-karat yellow gold, sterling silver, ebony, acrylic, wax, varnish;

hand constructed, laser engraved, inlaid, coated

Photo by Justin Malinowski

EDWARD LANE McCARTNEY

Ova-Rings, 2001

3.8 x 1.6 x 1.6 cm (each)

Fine silver, enamel; cold constructed

Photo by artist

ARIANE HARTMANN

The Best Place, 2003

3.4 x 3 x .3 cm (each)

Vinyl records, silver

Courtesy of Galerie V & V, Vienna, Austria

Photo by artist

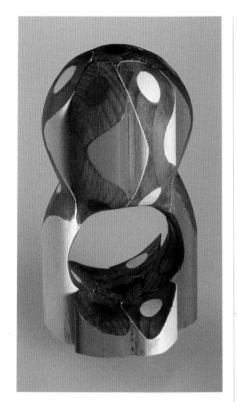

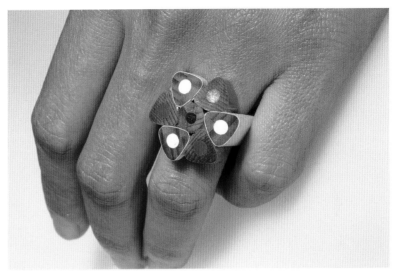

FERNANDO DeLAYE VILLALEVER

Day by Day, 1999

4 x 2.5 x 2 cm

Colored pencils; adhered, filed

Photos by Petra Jaschke

MASON DOUGLAS

Untitled, 2002

3.3 x .9 cm

Soda cans; compressed

Photo by artist

In the Victorian era, jewelry often held photographs of loved ones. I embraced that tradition in a personal ring capturing an image of my daughter.

Loretta Anne Castagna

LORETTA ANNE CASTAGNA

Eva by the Lake, 2003

3.3 x 2.8 x 2.5 cm

14-karat gold, 22-karat gold, sterling silver, photograph, resin, beach pebble, blue topaz; fabricated

Photo by artist

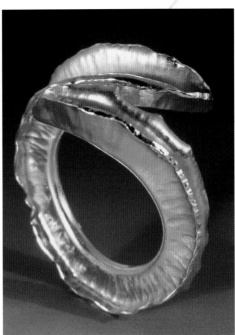

I love the evolutionary transformation—through hammering, persuasion, and struggle—from a flat sheet of metal toward an object of unity and fluidity. I enjoy the paradox that soft-looking metal may have required extreme force and skill to be produced.

Cynthia Eid

CYNTHIA EID

Floral Folded Ring I, 2001

2.5 x 2.5 x .6 cm

18-karat gold and sterling silver bimetal; fold formed

Photo by artist

ALAN REVERE

Up, Up, and Away, 2001

3.3 x 2.5 x 2.5 cm

18-karat yellow gold, 14-karat red gold, platinum, diamonds, ball bearing; fabricated, cast, set

Photo by Barry Blau

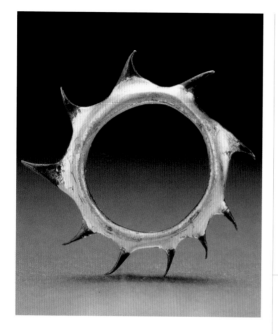

ANGELA GLEASON

Halo for St. Teresa of Calcutta:
Patroness of the Hungry and Poor, 2001
3.2 x 3.2 x .5 cm
Silver, 22-karat gold leaf, patina; cast
Photo by Hap Sakwa

MASUMI KATAOKA

Holding Onto One's Jewels, 2003
5 x 1.3 x 3 cm (each)
24-karat gold, 18-karat gold, copper, enamel,
human hair; electroformed, cast, soldered
Photo by artist

DONGCHUN LEE

Rings, 2003
2.7 x 3.2 x 2.9 cm (each)
Found iron sheet; cut, folded

ANNE BAEZNER

Dentelle (Lace), 1999

2 x 4 x 4 cm

Silver, silver chain mail

Photo by artist

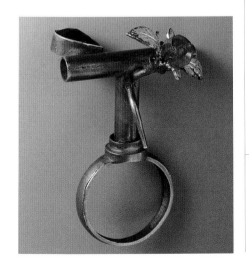

TONE VIGELAND

Ring III, 1981

4.5 x 2.2 x 1.6 cm

Steel, 14-karat gold, 18-karat gold, rusted steel

Photo by Hans-Jørgen Abel

KAROL WEISSLECHNER

Turnov, 2002

4.6 x 3 x 2.6 cm

Silver, Czechoslovakian

granite, gold leaf, patina

Photo by Pavol Janek

FELICITY PETERS

Nurture, 2002

4.2 x 4.3 x .8 cm

Lapis lazuli, sterling silver, 24-karat
gold; constructed, kum-boo

Photo by Victor France

KEITH E. LO BUE

Cupid's Revenge, 2003

3.8 x 3.8 x 2.5 cm

Sterling silver, steel, brass, raw opal, scissor handle,
glass lenses, eyeglass frame segment, screws,
engraving, soil; fabricated, assembled

Photo by Steve Rowson

PHILLIP BALDWIN

2 x 2, 1988

.6 x 2.5 x .2 cm (left)

Pattern-welded steel (mild steel and Monel®),

22-karat gold; bored, inlaid, soldered

Photo by artist

MARJORIE SCHICK

Ballycotton Bay, 2001

12.7 x 10.2 x 8.3 cm

Papier-mâché, paint,

metal, wood, cardboard

Photo by Gary Pollmiller

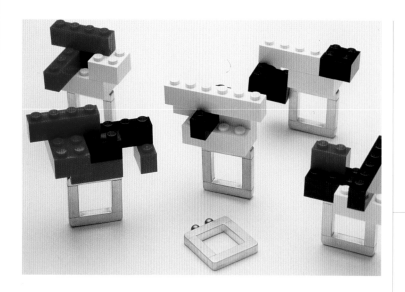

CINNAMON LEE

Acrylic Layer Rings, 2002

1.5 x 2.5 x 2.5 cm (each)

Acrylic, sterling silver, stainless steel;
hand machined, fabricated, riveted

Photo by artist

KATH INGLIS

Construction Rings, 2002

2.5 x 2.5 x .5 cm (each, base only)

Sterling silver, ball bearings, plastic toy building
bricks, rare earth magnets; cast, soldered

Photo by Michael Haines

GREG SIMS

Ace Diamonds, 2003

9 x 6 x 1.5 cm

Gold-plated base metal, diamond, playing
cards, packaging; cast, assembled

Photo by artist

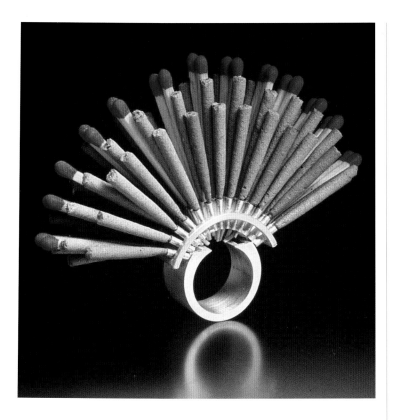

JOHN KENT GARROTT

Ignition Ring #1, 2003

7.6 x 5.7 x 1.3 cm

Sterling silver, matchsticks,

sparklers; hollow constructed

Photos by artist

KIMBERLY KEYWORTH

Three Rings, 2002

2.5 x 2.5 x 2.5 cm (each)

Sterling silver, 22-karat

gold, enamel; torch fired

Photo by George Post

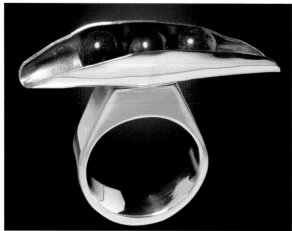

ROBERT COOGAN

Slider, 2002

3.8 x 3.8 x .9 cm

Sterling silver; fabricated,

box constructed

Photo by TTU Photo Services

MICHAEL BOYD

Poison Rings Group Shot, 2001
2.6 x 2.2 x 1.5 cm (each)
Sterling silver, 22-karat gold,
14-karat gold, precious stones,
semiprecious stones; fabricated
Photo by Tim Brown

ETSUKO SONOBE

Untitled, 2002
3.3 x 2.8 x 1.2 cm
20-karat gold, carnelian
Photo by Okinari Kurokawa

185

● **Like architectural landmarks in a city, I want my jewelry to capture attention. Each form is built as a small sculpture and is intended to engage the body as a stage for its display.**

Hye Seung Shin

HYE SEUNG SHIN

Geometric Rings, 2003

Various dimensions

Sterling silver

Photos by Myung-Wook Huh (Studio Munch)

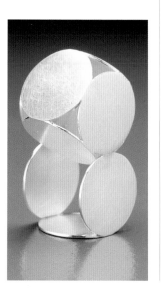

YAYO

Puzzle 13, 2001

3 x 2.6 x 1.5 cm

Sterling silver; cast, oxidized

Photos by artist

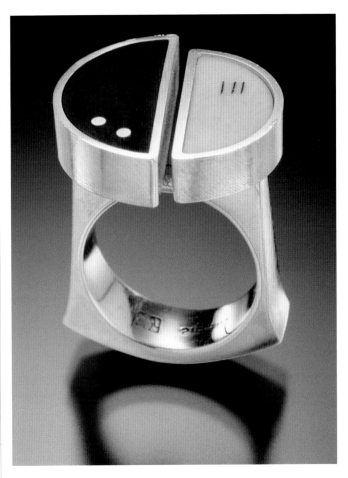

KRISTIN MITSU SHIGA

Modernismus I, 2002

2.5 x 2.2 x 2.2 cm

Sterling silver, ebony, piano key ivory

scrimshaw; cast, fabricated

Photo by Hap Sakwa

BRUNE BOYER PELLEREJ

Château en Espagne (Castle in the Air), 1996

3.3 x 2 x 1.5 cm

Silver, tourmaline; caning

Photos by Alfredo Rosado

SARA CILIA

Domed Ring 2, 2003

6 x 6 x .5 cm

Sterling silver, wire;

domed, soldered

Photo by artist

CLAUDE SCHMITZ

Rolling Ring, 2000

2.4 x 2.4 x 1.4 cm

Sterling silver

Photo by artist

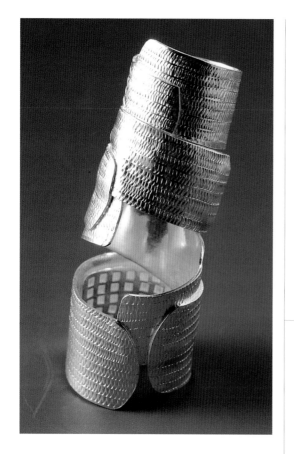

LAURENCE OPPERMANN

Muraille, 2001

1.5 x 2.8 cm

Silver

Photo by Sylvain Pretto

DANIEL HUYNH

Ring for a Broken Finger III, 2003

7.6 x 5 x 5 cm

Sterling silver;

fabricated, engraved

Photo by artist

JASON ALEXANDER

Pinhole Camera Ring #1, 2003

7 x 4 x 4 cm

Sterling silver, fine silver, black onyx,

brass shim stock; hinged

Photos by artist

DAN SAEGER

Magnifying Ring, 2001

3.8 x 2.5 x 1.3 cm

Sterling silver, blue topaz,

magnifying glass

Photo by artist

JENNIFER KELLOGG

Engagement Ring Box, 1993

3.8 x 2.5 x 1.3 cm

Sterling silver, cubic zirconia

Photo by artist

WINFRIED KRUEGER

Untitled, 1996
6 cm high
Silver, citrine
Photo by artist

RAÏSSA BUMP

Compliments, 2002
2.2 x 2.2 x 1.5 cm (each)
18-karat gold, sterling silver,
diamond crystals; cast, formed
Photo by Mark Johnston

LORI TALCOTT

Mardöll II, 2002

12 x 9.5 x 2.5 cm

Silver, 18-karat gold; fabricated

Photo by Douglas Yaple

CAROLINE v. STEINAU-STEINRÜCK

Ring, 1996

2.6 x 2.4 x 2.1 cm

18-karat gold; constructed

Photo by Eva Jünger

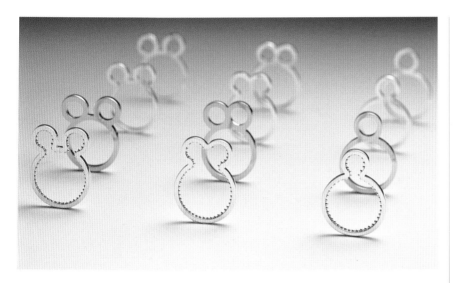

HWA-JIN KIM

+1, 2001

2.2 x 3.2 x .2 cm (each)

Sterling silver, gold plate

Photo by Nemo Studio

JESSE CONN

Curry Ring, 2002

4.4 x 2.2 x .9 cm

Sterling silver, gold plate,

copper, curry powder, cork;

hollow constructed,

chased, repoussé

Photo by Taweesak Molsawat

JASON MORRISSEY

Cuttlefish Cast Rings, 1999

3.2 x 2.5 x 2.5 cm (each)

Sterling silver, 14-karat gold;

cuttlefish cast

Photo by Robert Diamante

GINI ROLLINS

Temple Ring, 2002

5 x 3.2 x 1.6 cm

Sterling silver, 22-karat bimetal,

freshwater pearls; fabricated, engraved

Photo by artist

PAMELA MORRIS THOMFORD

Children of the Taliban, 2003

7.9 x 2.8 x 2.5 cm

Sterling silver, precious metal clay, bronze,
found brass mesh; cast, fired, fabricated

Photo by Tim Thayer

My production process is consciously unconscious, with elements being removed and added. The piece works best if I am both surprised and caught off guard. Then it has become itself all by itself. In this communication the piece finds its relevance and can regain its position in the subconscious as a possible answer to something human.

Ulrika Swärd

ULRIKA SWÄRD

Loneliness, 2001

6 x 4 x 2.5 cm

14-karat palladium white gold,

18-karat gold, silver

Photo by Castello Hansen/Ulrika Swärd

TRACY ROSE

Karma, 2003

2.5 x 2.5 x .8 cm

Titanium, stainless

steel balls; pressure fit

Photo by Hap Sakwa

● Combining the durability of
titanium with freely moving
stainless steel balls, this ring
design embodies a playful
seduction of movement, subtle
sound, and wearability.

Tracy Rose

EMI FUJITA

Offerings, 2003

7.5 x 8 x 3.5 cm

Glass; kiln cast, fused,

ground, assembled

Photo by Takeshi Noguchi

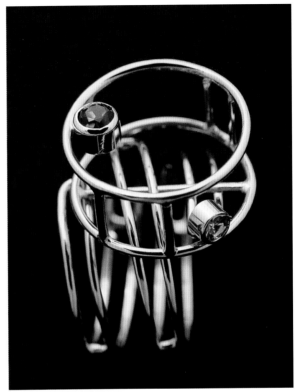

JENNIFER BROESKA

Armored Adornment, 2003

4 x 2.2 x 1 cm

Soda-lime glass, sterling silver;

lampworked, fabricated

Photo by Ken Mayer

MELINDA ALEXANDER

Round Ring, 2003

3.8 x 3.2 x 3.8 cm

14-karat white gold, amethyst,

garnet; constructed

Photo by Rob Romeo

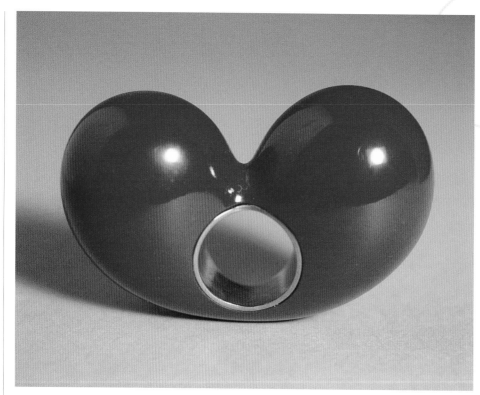

This series of rings was designed to be playful, sexy, and very dramatic. The forms are like fat cartoons, and they recall hearts, balloons, derrieres, and other erogenous zones. The colors, all variations of fire-engine red, are the colors of Eros.

Bruce Metcalf

BRUCE METCALF

Shankless Plump Red Ring, 2003

3.8 x 5.7 x 2.5 cm

Gold-plated silver, wood;

fabricated, carved, painted

Photo by artist

NORIKO HANAWA

Tea Time, 2003
4.4 x 2.6 x 2.3 cm (teapot);
3 x 2.2 x 1.7 cm (teacup);
2.4 x 2.7 x 1.7 cm (dish with fork)
Sterling silver, natural pearl;
hand fabricated
Photo by Federico Cavicchioli

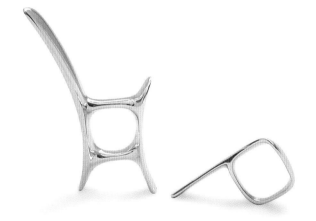

ON LUI

Sculptrings, 2003
6 x 3.2 x 1.5 cm (largest)
Sterling silver; wax carved,
cast, polished
Photo by Michael Pell

These pieces look at the negative space between fingers, knuckles, and the hand. They are meant to be worn or to stand freely as sculpture.

On Lui

STEVEN LUBECKI

Damascus Rings, 2003

2.5 x 2.2 x 1.9 cm (each)

Sterling silver, pattern-welded

Damascus steel cabochons;

forge welded, fabricated

Photo by Robert Diamante

CHRISTOPH ZELLWEGER

Ring, 1999

6 x 5 x 2 cm

Stainless steel; ceramic shell cast

Photo by artist

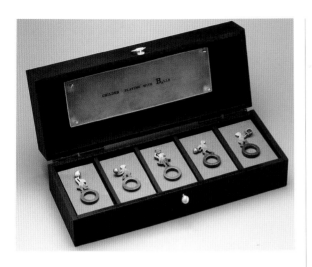

JI-YEON LIM

Playing, 2002

29 x 10 x 8 cm (boxed);

5.8 x 2.2 x .5 cm (each)

Silver, acrylic, plastic, fiberboard

Photos by Myung-Wook Huh

(Studio Munch)

KATH INGLIS

Catscradle Rings, 2002

3 x 3 x 2 cm (each)

Mild steel wire, white epoxy
paint; woven, knotted

Photo by Michael Haines

JENNIFER KELLOGG

Cage Rings, 2001

3.2 x 1.3 cm (each)

18-karat gold, uncut ruby

Photo by Luis Ernesto Santana

⦿ Often, it is the materials that can become inspiring, and sometimes, it is something else—something that draws you back for a second look. My focus is on creating jewelry that is both waggish and wearable as a personal adornment and a personal statement. The design is of much greater importance to me than the intrinsic value of its components.

Jennifer Kellogg

CHARLES LEWTON-BRAIN

Cage Ring: Stone B289, 2001

3 x 2.5 x 2.5 cm

Stainless steel wire, copper, 24-karat
gold, Nova Scotia beach stone;
fusion welded, electroformed

Photo by artist

LOLA BROOKS

Filigree Cocktail Rings, 2001

2.7 x 2.5 x 2.5 cm (average)

Stainless steel, champagne
rose cut diamonds, 18-karat
gold solder; constructed

Photo by Bob Barrett

RICHARD McCORMACK

Purple Passage 3, 2003

2.2 x 2.2 x 1.2 cm

Sterling silver, 22-karat bimetal,

18-karat bimetal, 22-karat gold,

amethyst; fabricated

Photo by Hap Sakwa

WHITNEY ABRAMS

Pegasus Ring, 2001

3.2 x 2.2 x 1.6 cm

22-karat gold, intaglio emerald,

ruby trillions, hessonite rose cut garnets;

hand carved, hand fabricated

Photo by Ralph Gabriner

ALAN PERRY

Wedding Ring, 1997

18-karat gold; rolled,
soldered, fabricated

Photo by Robert Diamante

KIM LUCCI-ELBUALY

Precious Series #1, 2001

3.2 x 2.5 x 1.3 cm

18-karat yellow gold, 14-karat
white gold, rutilated quartz;
fabricated, tension set

Photo by Ralph Gabriner

STEFANIE von SCHEVEN

Resin Ring, 2002

2 x 2 x .7 cm

Resin, platinum wire, pearl

Courtesy of Galerie V & V, Vienna, Austria

Photo by artist

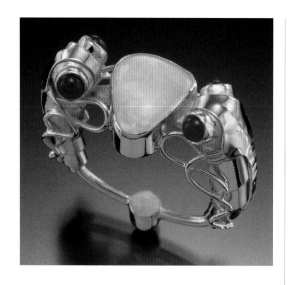

WILLIAM SCHOLL

Creature Ring, 2001

2.5 x 2.5 x 1.3 cm

18-karat yellow gold, rubies,
opal, sapphire; fabricated

Photo by Ralph Gabriner

KIM BUCK

Spell It Out, 2001

2 x 2 x .8 cm

18-karat gold; machine-milled
wax, lost wax cast

Photo by Ole Akhøj

KATHY BUSZKIEWICZ

Vanitati Sacrificium: Eternity, Fancy, Macho, 2000

.6 x 2.5 x 2.5 cm to 2.8 x 2.5 x 2.5 cm

18-karat gold, 14-karat gold,

U.S. currency, cubic zirconia; fabricated

Photo by artist

SUSAN WISE and JEFF WISE

Liquid Metal, 2000

2.5 x 2.5 x 1.9 cm

18-karat gold, platinum, sapphire,

opal, lapis lazuli; fabricated, inlaid

Photo by artists

KATHY BUSZKIEWICZ

Omnia Vanitas II, 2001

3.2 x 2.5 x 2.5 cm

18-karat gold, U.S. currency,

pearl; fabricated

Photo by artist

Spanish Scroll Ring, 2000 (left)

Leaf and Scroll Ring, 2002 (right)

3.2 x 2.5 cm (each)

18-karat yellow gold, ruby,

diamonds, platinum, sapphires;

cast, chased, pierced, engraved, set

Photo by Ralph Gabriner

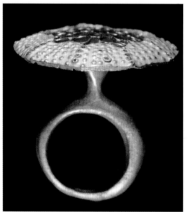

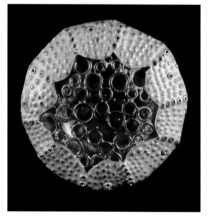

ALEXANDRA de SERPA PIMENTEL

Untitled, 2001

3.8 x 3.6 x 3.6 cm

Sterling silver, 19-karat gold, amber

beads; cuttlefish cast, fabricated

Photos by artist

Hands. We do so much with our hands without even a second thought. Hands find themselves in so many situations. In fact, the same hands that pierced, fit, filed, soldered, and finished this ring also enjoy wearing it!

Betsy Resnick

BETSY RESNICK

Spirit Stimulant, 2003

2.5 x 3.2 x 3.5 cm

Sterling silver, antique glass; hand fabricated

Photo by Douglas Yaple

DONOVAN WIDMER

Long Term Investment, 2001

6.4 x 7.6 x 2.5 cm

Sterling silver, brass, steel, coal,
found objects; fabricated

Photo by artist

My work is about the repetitive process of adding one part or one line after another and deciding my direction as I go along. It is kind of a meditative way to understand my feelings and emotions at the moment.

Yoko Shimizu

YOKO SHIMIZU

Alone, 2002

4 x 2 x 2 cm

Oxidized sterling silver,
18-karat gold; constructed

Photo by Federico Cavicchioli

MANUEL VILHENA

Untitled, 1999

3 x 2 x 1.5 cm

Oak, steel wood screws,
uncut olivine; dyed

Photo by Rob Turner

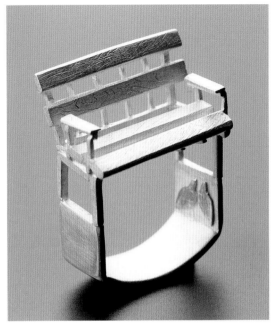

J. RUDIGER LORENZEN

Handschmuck, 2002

3.5 x 4 x 2.5 cm

Steel, silver, enamel; constructed

Photo by Petra Jaschke

JOHANNA BECKER-BLACK

Park Bench and Pigeons, 2003

3 x 2 x 1 cm

Sterling silver, 22-karat gold;

fabricated, constructed

Photo by Federico Cavicchioli

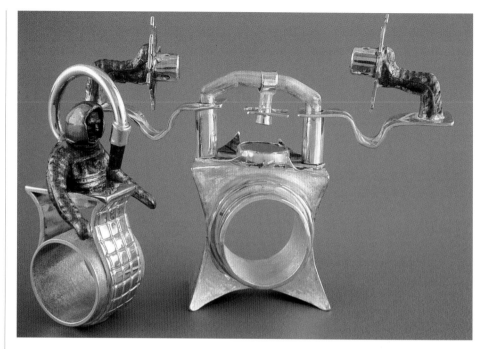

CAROLINE MILLER

Captain Dan & Captain Dan's Legs, 2002

3.8 x 2.5 x 1.9 cm (left);

7.6 x 8.9 x 1.9 cm (right)

Sterling silver, bronze, magnets,

sunstone; cast, constructed

Photo by artist

JUDY WENIG-HORSWELL

Trophy Ring V, 2003

4.4 x 3.2 x 1.3 cm

Sterling silver; lost wax cast

Photo by Eric A. Nisly

KERI ATAUMBI

Boar Walking, 2002

3.8 x 3.2 x 1.3 cm

Silver; lost wax cast

Photo by James Hart

TODD TURNER

Teapot Ring, 1995

2.9 x 1.3 x 2.1 cm

Sterling silver, 18-karat yellow gold;

hand fabricated, soldered, polished

Photo by artist

TODD TURNER

Teacup Ring, 1995

3 x 1.3 x 2.2 cm

Sterling silver; hand fabricated,

soldered, sandblasted

Photo by artist

● Message rings are instant jewelry. They are made as a reaction to the communication that is going on in a specific moment.

Claudia Stebler

CLAUDIA STEBLER

Message on Your Body, 2001

2 x 2 x 1 cm

Plastic labels; machined

Photo by Petra Jaschke

FELIEKE van der LEEST

Pom-pom Rings, 1999

3 x 3 x 2 cm (each)

Polyester/polyamide textile,

pom-poms; knitted

Photo by artist

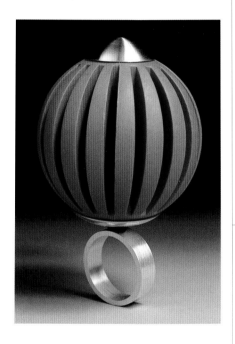

ROBLY A. GLOVER

K9-2, 2003

8.9 x 6.4 x 6.4 cm

Rubber, sterling silver;

constructed

Photo by artist

SHELLEY NORTON

Untitled, 2001

Various dimensions

Monofilament, beads, sequins,

plastic drink lid, sterling silver,

semiprecious gemstones,

22-karat yellow gold;

hand woven, bezel set

Photo by John Collie

How we make meaning endlessly fascinates me. By making pieces that are colorful and have a humorous appeal, I want the viewer and the wearer to engage with the work; to experience the type of feeling one has being at a fancy dress party; and, with the suspension of reality these types of occasions create, become aware of new ways of seeing and thinking.

Shelley Norton

HEATHER WHITE

Circle Ring: Pet, 2002

6.4 x 6.4 x 2.2 cm

Gold, sterling silver, fur;

constructed

Photo by Dean Powell

JOSÉE DESJARDINS

Untitled, 2002

5.8 x 2.8 x 2.8 cm

Sterling silver, sheep's wool, dog hair;

felted, lost wax cast, constructed

Photo by Paul Simon

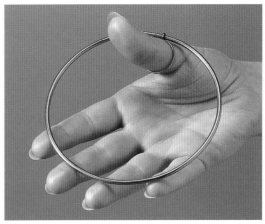

SHANA ASTRACHAN

Orange Felted Ring, 2003

2.5 x 1.6 x .3 cm

Oxidized sterling silver, silk, mohair;

knotted, wrapped, felted

Photo by Chris McCaw

NATHALIE GOULIART

Anneau de Parole (A Ring to Speak), 2002

11.2 x 11.2 x .3 cm

Copper, patina; fired

Photo by Aline Princet

KRISTIE REISER

Cotton Ball Ring #2, 2001

5 x 3.2 x 3.2 cm

Sterling silver, cotton ball;

riveted, constructed

Photo by Jim Wildeman

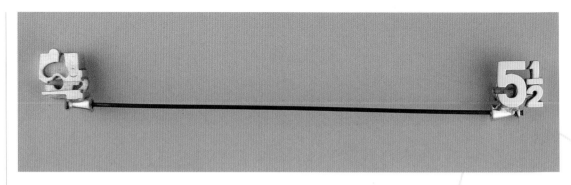

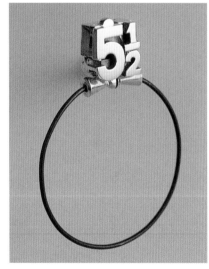

● I search for contemporary developments in high technology and mechanization that are not adverse to the format of jewelry; that open new ways into previously unattainable levels of interaction between beauty, physicality, and knowledge. I feel this approach is especially potent in the ring format, where the connection between the flesh and metal is the most direct.

Sergey Jivetin

SERGEY JIVETIN

5 1/2 Ring, 2003

3.2 x 2.5 x .6 cm

18-karat gold, nickel titanium wire

Photos by artist

In this ring, I like the tension created by the two cutlets almost touching each other. I also enjoy dispelling traditional jewelry design notions of how something is supposed to be done. Some people may think I set the two diamonds "upside down" or the "wrong way."

Abrasha

ABRASHA

Machined Ring #4, 2000
2.6 x 2.1 x .5 cm
Stainless steel, 18-karat gold, diamonds; machined, fabricated, cold connected, riveted
Photo by Ronnie Tsai

Solitary is meant to be a prototype model for an extruded tube with this specific solitaire shape. You saw off a piece of the tube, as much as the customer wants, polish, price, and sell it!

Marcel van Kan

MARCEL van KAN

Solitary, 2000
3.5 x 1.9 x .9 cm
Stainless steel; bent, single solder
Photo by Ted Noten

THERESA SAMANIEGO

Finger Trap, 2002

8.9 x 7.6 x 2.5 cm

Sterling silver

Photo by Rachelle Thiewes

HEE JOO KIM

Relaxation, 2003

13 x 4.5 x 2 cm

Sterling silver

Photo by Myung-Wook Huh (Studio Munch)

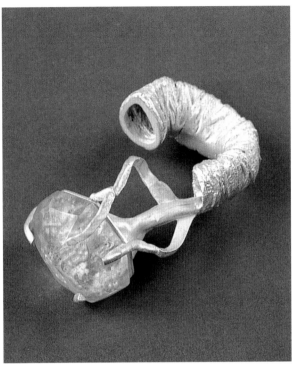

JOELLE KING

Knuckles, BC, 2003

5 x 5.4 x 1.9 cm

Sterling silver; fabricated

Photos by Gina Rymarcsuk

ANDREA WAGNER

Untitled, 1999

3.5 x 3.5 x 6 cm

Silver, epoxide resin, gold pigment;

cast, set, faceted

Photo by artist

● A fascination with ancient Greek and Roman jewelry is evident in my design. Each piece is hand fabricated after I alloy the gold, mill the sheet, and pull the wire. By using the ancient technique of granulation it's as if history is repeating itself, and I can be a part of that history.

Jill Hurant

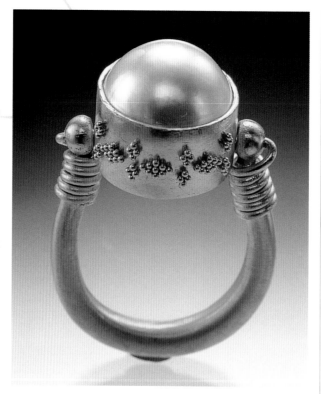

JILL HURANT

Untitled, 2002

3.2 x 1.9 x 1.3 cm

22-karat gold, mabe pearl;
hand fabricated, granulated

Photo by Ralph Gabriner

JOHANNES KUHNEN

Ring, 1991

2.7 x 2.8 x .7 cm

18-karat gold, Monel®

Photo by artist

● Geometry, simplicity, function, and usage play important roles in my metal pieces. I use sterling silver to minimize the color and give a simple elegance that focuses on the composition and the design elements.

Hye-Jeong Ko

HYE-JEONG KO

Ring, 2001

2.5 x 2.5 x 1.3 cm

Sterling silver, 22-karat bimetal

Photo by Dan Neuberger

PATRICIA TELESCO

Pearl Ring, 2001

2.2 x .8 cm

18-karat palladium white gold, 18-karat

yellow gold, pearl; cast, fabricated

Courtesy of Mobilia Gallery,

Cambridge, Massachusetts

Photo by Randy Batista

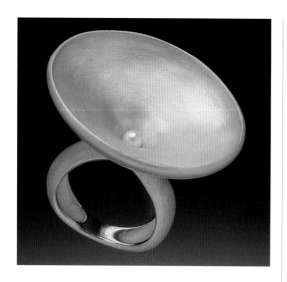

HEATHER WHITE

Broaching Ring #2, 2002

3.2 x 2.5 x 3.2 cm

18-karat gold, seed pearl

Photo by Dean Powell

CHIHIRO MAKIO

Shell Flower Ring, 2003

3.8 x 3.8 x 3.8 cm

Mother of pearl button, glass beads,

thread, oxidized sterling silver

Photo by Ivo M. Vermeulen

PAZ FERNÁNDEZ

Transformation, 2001

3.2 x 2.5 x 2.5 cm

Sterling silver, 18-karat gold,

22-karat gold, steel beads;

cast, fabricated

Photo by Peter Groesbeck

JENN PARNELL

Single Eddy Ring with Pearl, 2001

1.3 cm in diameter

Sterling silver, opalescent enamel,

cultured freshwater pearl; fabricated,

lost wax cast, kiln fired

Photo by Mark Johnston

MICHAEL BOYD

Untitled, 2003

3 x 2.2 x 2.5 cm

18-karat gold, 22-karat gold,
emerald, black sapphire, green
aquamarine, citrine; fabricated

Photo by Tim Brown

JODI JOHNSON

Northwest Traditions #3, 2003

3.8 x 3.5 x 1.9 cm

18-karat gold; fabricated, cast

Photo by Richard Nicol

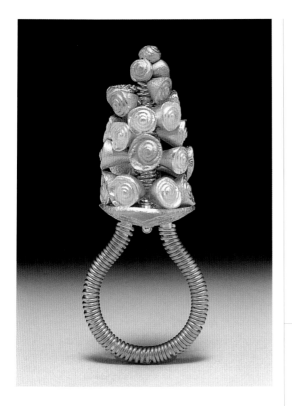

KATHLEEN BROWNE

Tower, 2000

5 x 2.5 x 2.5 cm

Fine silver, sterling silver, 24-karat gold,

precious metal clay; cast, fabricated

Photo by artist

STEVE COMBS

Ring from the *Past and Present* series, 2003

3.2 x 1.9 x 1.3 cm

Sterling silver, antique

mother-of-pearl button; fabricated

Photo by Cynda O'Brien

IDA FORSS

Teeth, 2002

3 x 2.5 x .8 cm

18-karat gold, Corian®; engraved

Photo by artist

THERESE HILBERT

Vessel Rings, 1999

3.8 x 2.6 cm (left); 4.8 x 2.6 cm (right)

Sterling silver

Photo by Otto Künzli

ETSUKO SONOBE

Untitled, 2000

2.3 x 2.3 x 1.9 cm

20-karat gold

Photo by Okinari Kurokawa

JANICE DERRICK

Set of Two Moving Rings with Flat Elements, 2001

2.5 x 2 x 4 cm

Sterling silver, oxidized silver,

9-karat yellow gold; fabricated, pierced,

scored, folded, soldered, forged

Photo by Joël Degan

SUE LORRAINE

Removal of the Stone of Folley, 2001

2.5 x 2.5 x 1.5 cm

Pure gold, lead; embossed

Photo by Grant Hancock

HATTIE SANDERSON

Electroformed Ring, 2002

2.5 x 2.5 x 2.5 cm

Sterling silver, electroformed copper,

polymer clay, dichroic glass,

24-karat gold plate, silver plate

Photo by artist

GIANCARLO MONTEBELLO

Cartiglio, 1996

2.5 x 2 x 2 cm

18-karat yellow gold, enamel,

amethyst cabochon

Photo by Ruggero Boschetti

SABINE KLARNER

Tiger and Dragon, 2003

3.5 x 4 x 3 cm

Silver, gold, precious stones,

photo, miniature sword

Photo by Katrin Gauditz

CASTELLO HANSEN

Untitled, 2001

4 x 2.1 x 1.2 cm

18-karat gold, reconstructed coral

Photo by artist

ELIZABETH McDEVITT

Ivy Leaves, 2001

2.5 x 2.5 x 1.3 cm

22-karat gold, Australian black crystal opal;

hand formed, chased, repoussé

Photo by Keith Roberts

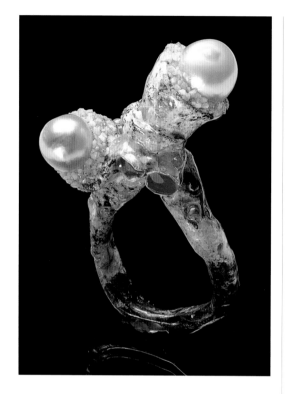

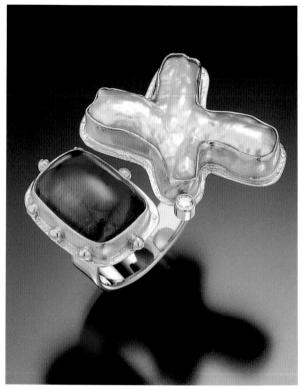

TOMOMI ARATA

Treasures from Under the Sea, 2003

4.3 x 3 x 2 cm

Silver, enamel, sand, pearl; hand cast

Photo by Minoru Hashimoto

ISABELLE POSILLICO

Hug, Kiss With a Spark, 2002

2.8 x 1.9 x 1.9 cm

14-karat gold, 18-karat gold, 22-karat gold,
rhodolite garnet, pearl, diamond; hand
formed, constructed, soldered, textured, set
Photo by Hap Sakwa

THOMAS DAILING
Untitled, 2001
2.6 x 2.2 x 1.2 cm
Chrome tourmaline (concave
faceted by Richard Homer),
diamonds, 18-karat
yellow gold; cast
Photo by Azad

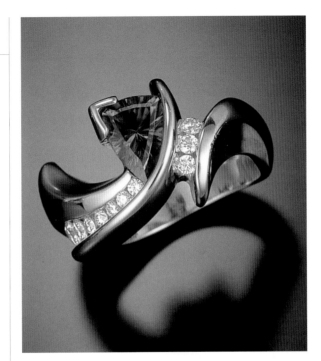

KLAUS BÜRGEL
Untitled, 2001
3.3 x 4.1 x 2.1 cm
18-karat gold, garnets;
cast, fabricated
Photo by Mark Johnston

235

ALINE KOKINOPOULOS

Queribus Castle, 2003

3 x 2.5 x 2 cm

Silver, amethyst, tourmaline,

rubies, citrine; wax carved, cast

Photo by Jean-Christophe Lett

JEFFERY E. TAYLOR

Untitled, 2001

7.6 x 7.6 x 2.8 cm

Tagua nut, silver, shoe-brush bristles;

carved, constructed

Photo by artist

JIN-HEE JUNG

Swing Swing Rings, 2003

4 x 4 x 3.5 cm (on hand)

Silver, copper

Photos by Myung-Wook Huh

(Studio Munch)

BEVERLY PENN

Locus: the Spirit of Place, 2003

8.9 x 8.9 x 3.2 cm

18-karat gold, oxidized

sterling silver; etched

Photo by Christopher Zaleski

KRISTINA S. KADA

Tamago Rings, 2001

2.8 x 2.5 x 1.9 cm (each)

Sterling silver, 22-karat gold

bimetal, patina, lacquer;

hand fabricated,

hollow constructed

Photo by Hap Sakwa

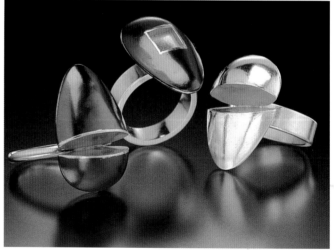

Tamago is the Japanese word for egg. I am drawn to the egg shape. The lines are soft and gradual. To me, the egg symbolizes birth, a new beginning. It also reminds me of the connection between a mother and her baby.

Kristina S. Kada

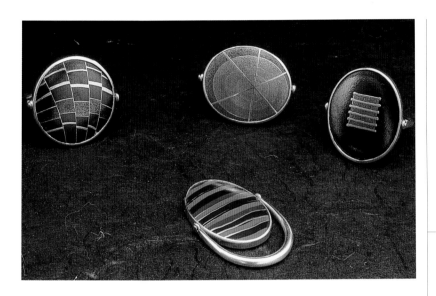

DEBORAH KRUPENIA

Swivel Rings, Rhythmical: Four Variations, 2001

2.2 x 1.9 cm (largest bead)

Japanese copper alloys (shakudo,

kuromi-do, shibuichi), 22-karat colored

gold, 18-karat colored gold, sterling silver,

patina; married metals, fabricated, etched

Photo by Dean Powell

JI-HEE HONG

Balance, 2003

2.8 x 2.5 x 1 cm

Sterling silver

Photo by Kwang-Chun Park

(KC Studio)

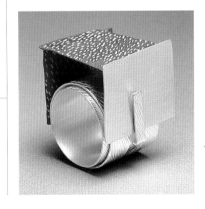

HYUNG-LAN CHOI

Small Object, 2003

2.5 x 2.3 x 2.8 cm

Silver, copper

Photo by Myung-Wook Huh

(Studio Munch)

JANTJE FLEISCHHUT

Nylon Rings, 1998

1.5 x 2.5 cm (each)

Fishing line; dyed, crocheted

Photo by Lucas Peters Photography

CLAUDE WESEL

Galet, 1998

3 x 2 x 3 cm

18-karat gold

Photo by Lucien Krauss

ANNE BAEZNER

Buisson (Bush), 1999

3.5 x 2.7 x 2.7 cm

Gold, patinated brass

Photo by artist

ESTEFÂNIA R. de ALMEIDA

Covo Ring, 2003

3 x 3 x 2.2 cm

18-karat gold

Photo by Carmen Graça

HILDE DE DECKER

For the Farmer and the Gardener, 1997–2003

Variable dimensions

Silver, vegetables

Photo by artist

MARY SCHIMPFF-WEBB

Untitled, 2000

1.3 x 1.3 x 1.9 cm

Sterling silver, 14-karat yellow gold,

blue onyx, coral, clear quartz, ruby

Photo by artist

MAJA

Surprise, 2003

3.2 x 2.5 x 2.5 cm

Sterling silver, cultured pearl;

fabricated, textured, oxidized

Photo by Hap Sakwa

JAN PETERS

Ring with Pearl, 2000

1.6 x 2.2 x .6 cm

Sterling silver, 14-karat gold,

cultured Japanese pearl, neoprene;

fabricated, filed, burnished

Photo by Ralph Gabriner

SHAVA LAWSON

Orange Button Ring, 2003

2.5 x 2.5 x 2.5 cm

Found button, sterling silver;

fabricated, riveted

Photo by Douglas Yaple

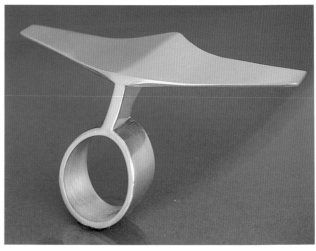

ERIK TIDÄNG

Silverwing, 2003

3.3 x 3.5 x 7.4 cm

Silver

Photo by artist

TAWEESAK MOLSAWAT

Why?, 2003

10.2 x 4.4 x 4.4 cm

Sterling silver, model globe, pencil,

eraser, patina; fabricated

Photo by artist

TAMARA CLARK

Starry Galaxy, 2003

2.7 x 2 x 3 cm

Sterling silver, 18-karat gold,

star sapphire; hand forged, hammered

Photo by Hans Sipma

SEO YOON CHOI

A Finger Plays, 2000

15 x 2 x 3 cm

Sterling silver, stainless steel

Photo by Myung-Wook Huh

(Studio Munch)

JACQUELINE RYAN

Untitled, 2002

2.4 x 1.5 cm

18-karat gold; pierced, soldered

Photo by Giovanni Corvaja

JACLYN DAVIDSON

Sybil Ring, 2002

2.5 x .6 x .6 cm

18-karat gold, pearl; fabricated,

hand carved, cast, chased, filed,

engraved, polished, set

Photo by Ralph Gabriner

MADELEINE WESTON LEWIS

Crane, 2001

3.1 x 2.5 x 2.4 cm

22-karat gold, South Sea mabe pearl;

hand cast, finished

Photo by Ralph Gabriner

EMMA FARQUHARSON

Spiral Cone Ring, 2002

3.5 x 2.3 x 2 cm

18-karat gold; formed,

hand fabricated, cast

Photo by Ralph Gabriner

EVA I. WERNER

Ring with Green Tourmaline, 2003

2.5 x 1.5 x 1.2 cm

18-karat yellow gold,

green tourmaline; constructed,

interconnected, soldered, set

Photo by Peter White

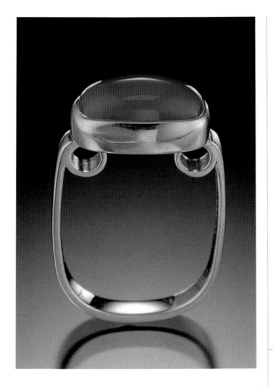

BABETTE von DOHNANYI

Crystal Ring, 2001

2 x 2 x 1.2 cm

18-karat gold; cast, surface treated

Photo by Federico Cavicchioli

BETSY BENSEN

Untitled, 2001

2.5 x 1.9 x .6 cm

18-karat gold, 14-karat gold,

holly blue agate; fabricated

Photo by Hap Sakwa

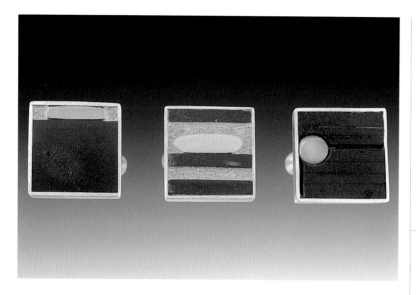

TERRI LOGAN

Slate & Rock Series, 2003

2.5 x 2.5 x 1.3 cm

Sterling silver, slate, rock, concrete,

patina; constructed, cast, inlaid

Photo by Jerry Anthony

SABINE AMTSBERG

Untitled, 2002

.7 x 2.5 x 3.1 cm

Sterling silver, copper; mokume gane,

fabricated, hollow constructed

Photo by Christoph Papsch

FLORENCE CROISIER

Destins Croisés, 2000

1.5 cm in diameter (largest)

Silver, gold; cut, soldered

Photo by artist

TODD REED

Diamond Grid Ring, 2002

1.9 x 1.9 x .6 cm

18-karat yellow gold, 22-karat yellow gold, sterling silver, cut diamonds, natural uncut diamond cubes, patina; forged, fabricated, brushed finish

Photo by Azad

BARBARA HEATH

Fox Ring, 1992

2 x 2.2 x 2.4 cm

18-karat gold, diamonds,

antique hand-painted enamel

button; wax carved, cast

Photo by Peter Budd

ALAN ARDIFF

Now You See It..., 2003

3 x 2.3 x .8 cm

18-karat yellow gold, 18-karat

white gold, sapphire

Photos by Michael Blake

MARY LEWIS

Out of Reach, 2003

6.4 x 2.5 x 2.5 cm

Sterling silver, stainless steel,

24-karat gold, rubber, patina;

cast, hand fabricated, kum-boo

Photo by Dan Neuberger

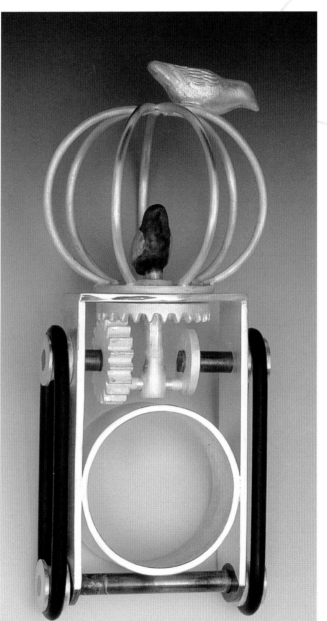

When the wearer rolls this ring across a flat surface, the movement of the gears turn the birdcage, and the movement of the cam makes the bird inside of the cage move up and down in a circular motion, all simultaneously.

Mary Lewis

HEE-KYUNG SHIN

Chess Rings II, 1997
3.6 x 3.6 x .7 cm (largest ring);
.1 x 48 x 48 cm (board)
Sterling silver, cat's-eye,
etched nickel silver, silicon
Photos by Kwang-Chun Park
(KC Studio)

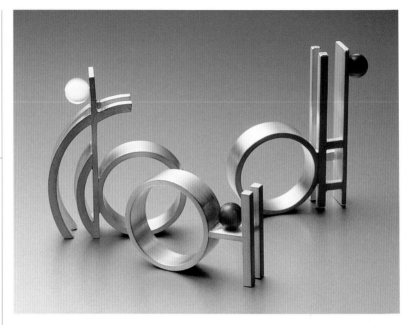

ESTHER DAVIES

The Tabernacle, 2002

6.4 x 12.7 x 2.5 cm

Sterling silver, 14-karat gold, 18-karat gold,

gemstones; fabricated, cut, formed,

soldered, hinged, set

Photo by Hap Sakwa

THEA IZZI

Fiore Futuristico, 2001

3.8 x 1.3 x 3.4 cm

Sterling silver and 22-karat gold bimetal,

hematite bead; hand fabricated

Photo by Hap Sakwa

S. C. BROWN

Untitled, 2001

1 x 2.1 x 2.3 cm

18-karat yellow gold, pink tourmaline,
diamond; cast, fabricated, bezel set

Photo by Hap Sakwa

● I like anything medieval and I like asymmetry. Some of my favorite designs mix the two styles. They make old art new, and the new art seems to have a soul.

S. C. Brown

REGINE SCHWARZER

Two Fingerrings, 2002

3.5 x 4.2 x 1.9 cm

Sterling silver, 22-karat gold, prehnite,
amethyst, opal, chrysoprase

Photo by Grant Hancock

BEATE KLOCKMANN

Blue Ring, 2002

4.5 x 4 x 4 cm

Gold, silver, enamel; hammered,

milled, folded, soldered

Photo by artist

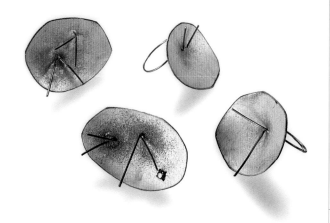

MARTINA MÜHLFELLNER

Bacini di'Aqua e di Fuoco (Pools of Water and Fire), 2003

2 x 3 x 3 cm

Sterling silver, 18-karat white gold,

enamel, granite; constructed

Photo by Federico Cavicchioli

DAPHNE KRINOS

Rings 2, 2002

3 x .5 x 1 cm

18-karat gold, aquamarine beads

Photo by Joël Degen

My work explores the quiet elegance found in things often overlooked or taken for granted, the idea that transcendence can be found in what's common and small, and that that awareness and appreciation can create a mysterious and strange beauty.

Deborrah Daher

DEBORRAH DAHER

Two, 2002

1.6 x 1.9 x .3 cm

Boulder opals, 22-karat yellow gold, 18-karat yellow gold, 14-karat yellow gold; fabricated

Photo by artist

RICHARD PALERMO
for COLOR CRAFT

Modern Man's Ring, 2002

2.4 x 2.2 x .9 cm

18-karat rose gold, white gold, princess cut diamond; constructed, burnish set

Photo by Michael Cuiccio

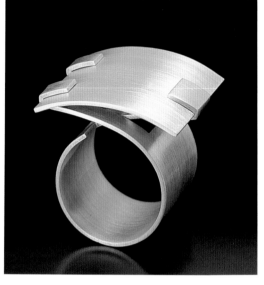

MICHAL BAR-ON

Marriage #2, 1998

5 x 3.7 x .03 cm (right)

22-karat gold, 24-karat gold foil, silver;

hand cut, mill rolled, die formed

Photo by Shmaya Cohen

JULIA TURNER

Tension Ring #1, 2001

2.8 x 2.5 x 2.5 cm

Sterling silver; fabricated

Photo by artist

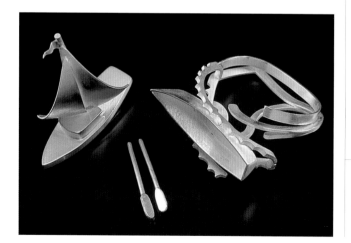

DAVID KISSEL

Boat Ring, 2000

8.2 x 5 x 3.8 cm

Sterling silver; fabricated

Photo by Helen Shirk

DAVID VROOMAN

#18, from the *Phoenix Series*, 2003

2 x 1.5 x 2 cm

22-karat gold, 18-karat gold, oxidized
sterling silver, freeform fire agate;
hand fabricated, fused

Photo by Nissa Vrooman

SUE LORRAINE

Ceremonial Rings, 1989

4.5 x 4 x 2.2 cm (each)

Concrete, gold leaf, mild
steel; cast, fabricated

Photo by Michael Kluvanek

ANDY COOPERMAN

Tension Orbit Ring, 2003

3.2 x 2.4 cm

Sterling silver, 18-karat gold, titanium
bearing, yellow diamond; forged,
fabricated, tension set

Photo by Douglas Yaple

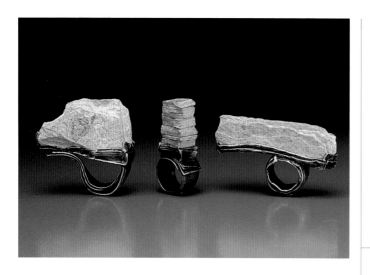

SEUNG JIN LEE

Impression, 2002

5 x 5.2 x 1.2 cm (left); 4 x 2.3 x 1.8 cm (center);

3.6 x 6.9 x 1 cm (right)

Silver, fish fossil; wax cast

Photo by Myung-Wook Huh (Studio Munch)

AGNES KAINZ

Untitled, 2002

4.5 x 4 x 2 cm

Brazilian rosewood; carved

Photo by artist

● **I aim to encapsulate bodies in motion. I use carved wood for flowing shapes because of its sensuality and its warm and soft characteristics. I make wooden rings because I enjoy the touch of wood on skin.**

Agnes Kainz

LINDA THREADGILL

Tudor Rose Ring, 2002

10.2 x 10.2 cm (base)

Sterling silver, 18-karat gold, wood;

constructed, cast

Photo by James Threadgill

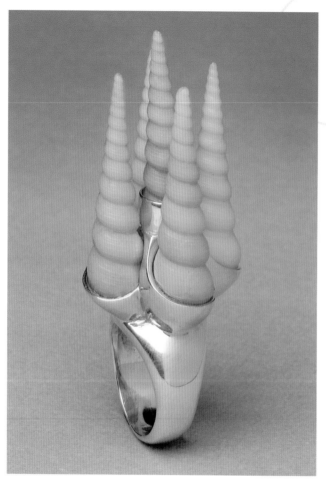

PIERRE CAVALAN

Sueño en la Playa, 2003

6.5 x 3.5 x 3.5 cm

Silver, shells

Photo by Steve Rowson

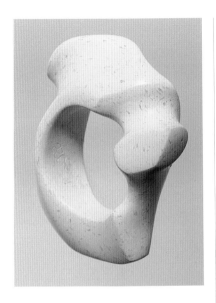

ANDREW GOSS

Bone, 2003

4.6 x 3.6 x 1.5 cm

Concrete (white portland cement,

limestone dust); carved

Photo by artist

ROBIN QUIGLEY

Eggs I & II, 2001

1.9 x 3.2 x 3.2 cm (left); 3.3 x 2.5 x 3.8 cm (right)

Silver, porcelain shard

Courtesy of Mobilia Gallery,

Cambridge, Massachusetts

Photo by Mark Johnston

NANCY MOYER

Burning at Both Ends Ring, 2002

3.8 x 3.8 x 1.9 cm (each)

Sterling silver, garnet cabochons,

rubber; fabricated, soldered, set

Photo by Robert Diamante

WESLEY GLEBE

Finger Rings, 2003

2.2 x .5 x 2.2 cm (each)

Titanium, 24-karat gold, stainless steel,

platinum; cold connected

Photo by Michael Black

JOANNA GOLLBERG

Hollow Ring, 2000

3.2 x 3.2 x 2.5 cm

Sterling silver, nickel silver;

married metal, fabricated,

hollow form constructed

Photo by Seth Tice-Lewis

JIŘÍ ŠIBOR

Ring, 2002

4.4 cm in diameter

Stainless steel; constructed,

cold connected, riveted

Courtesy of Galerie V & V, Vienna, Austria

Photo by Miroslav Zavadil, Bc.

STUART CATHEY

LV, 2002

2 x 2.2 x 2.7 cm

18-karat gold, rock crystal;

cast, fabricated

Photos by Robert Diamante

VEERLE VAN WILDER

She, from the series *1001 Arabian Nights Twice Over*, 2002
2.5 x 5 x 1 cm
18-karat yellow gold, rubies, diamonds; hand forged, partly polished, partly sandblasted
Photo by Luc Van Muylem

VEERLE VAN WILDER

He, from the series *1001 Arabian Nights Twice Over*, 2002
2.8 x 2.4 x 1.5 cm
18-karat yellow gold, brown diamond; hand formed, plated, partly polished, partly sandblasted
Photo by Luc Van Muylem

KLAUS BÜRGEL

Untitled, 2000
4.4 x 3.2 x 2.3 cm
18-karat gold; hollow constructed
Photo by Mark Johnston

JERI KAPLAN

Enchanting, 2002

2.5 x .9 cm

14-karat gold, hexagon citrine,

diamonds; prong set

Photo by Michael Knott

MIRJAM BUTZ-BROWN

Sunrise, 1997

3 x .9 x 2.3 cm

18-karat yellow gold, lapis lazuli,

yellow sapphires; wax cast,

hand fabricated

Photo by Jeff Scovil

ANDREA WIPPERMANN

Ring, 1994

4.5 x 3.5 cm

Gold, silver; cast

Photo by André Geßner

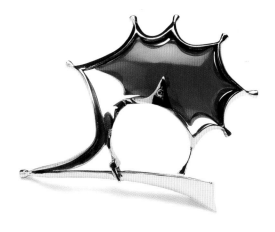

PAUL LEATHERS

Inorganic Roadkill, 1994

2.5 x 2.3 x 2.5 cm

18-karat yellow gold,

rubellite; cast

Photo by artist

SERGEY BOGDANOV

Untitled, 2003

4 x 5 cm

18-karat yellow gold, synthetic ruby,

diamonds; carved

Photo by Joël Degen

MIWHA OH

Born Again, 2000

3.2 x 2.5 x .6 cm

Steel, 24-karat gold, diamond;

formed, soldered, cast, set

Photo by Myung-Wook Huh

(Studio Munch)

KATHLEEN BROWNE

Luna, 2001

5 x 3.8 x 3.8 cm

Fine silver, sterling silver, 24-karat
gold, 18-karat gold, precious
metal clay; cast, fabricated

Photo by artist

JACK and ELIZABETH GUALTIERI
ZAFFIRO GOLDSMITHING

Chiara Ring, 1999

2.5 x 2.5 x 3.2 cm

22-karat yellow gold, platinum,
18-karat yellow gold, tanzanite;
hand fabricated, torch-fusion granulated

Photo by Daniel Van Rossen

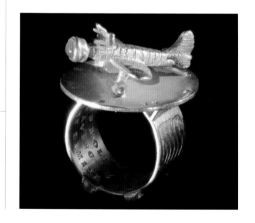

PAUL PRESTON

Red Mole Leaving Care Behind, 1993

3.2 cm high

18-karat gold, red gold, fine
gold, pink ruby; burnish set

Photo by Chris Bowerman

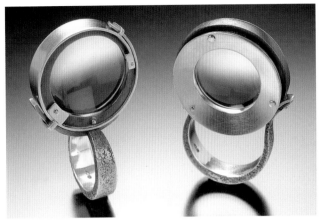

ANDY COOPERMAN

Two Finger Loupes, 2003

5 cm high (each)

Sterling silver, 7x lenses, 18-karat gold,

14-karat gold, bronze

Photo by Douglas Yaple

YURI NA

Rings for Filtering I: On the Water, 2003

5 x 4 x 3 cm (each)

Silver, copper, ammonite,

pearl; hand constructed

Photo by artist

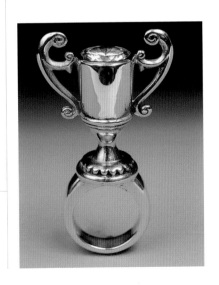

ELISSA B. STEINERT

Wedding Ring for a Trophy Wife, 2003

6.4 x 3.8 x 1.9 cm

Brass, cubic zirconia

Photo by Robly A. Glover

DEE FONTANS

Cosmetic Jewellery, 2001
4.4 x 2.5 x 8.8 cm
Sterling silver, garnets, enamel,
mirror; soldered, constructed,
tube set, pressure fit
Photo by Charles Lewton-Brain

ABIGAIL SAAK

Staple Yourself, 2003
2.5 x 2.5 x 7.6 cm (top);
3.8 x 1.9 x 1.9 cm (bottom)
Silver, stainless steel
found parts, velvet; cast
Photo by Frank Flood

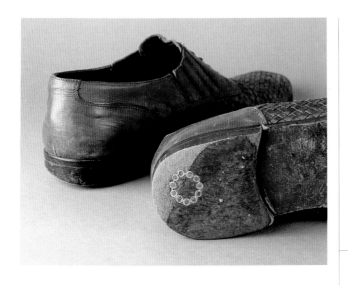

GITTA PIELCKE

Mozart and His Family, 2001

2.8 x 2.8 x .7 cm

Post cards, chocolate wrapper

Courtesy of Galerie V & V, Vienna, Austria

Photo by artist

GISBERT STACH

Firestep, 1994

2.4 x 2.4 x .7 cm (ring)

18-karat gold, flints, shoes;

embedded

Photo by artist

● A golden ring in the shape of a revolver magazine is attached to the heel of a shoe as if the wearer inadvertently stepped on it. Instead of bullets, there are crude flint stones incorporated into the ring so that the wearer performs a sparking walk. On his way, he leaves a practically imperceptible golden trace.

Gisbert Stach

BIBA SCHUTZ

Seeds, 2003

2.3 x 3.5 x .7 cm (left);

2.8 x 2.1 x .8 cm (right)

Sterling silver, fine silver; oxidized,

textured, wrapped, beaded, constructed

Photo by Ron Boszko

HANA PAIK

Movable Rings, 2002

4.2 x 4.5 x .8 cm (left); 6.2 x 6.1 x .8 cm (rear);

6.1 x 2.3 x .9 cm (right)

Sterling silver; hollow constructed

Photo by artist

PAVEL HERYNEK

Ring for the Finger, 2001

3.7 x 1.9 x 3.1 cm

Bottle cap, felt, stainless steel

Courtesy of Galerie V & V, Vienna, Austria

Photo by Markéta Ondrusková

SONIA MOREL

Substitution, 2003

6 x 5 x 5 cm

Silver; oxidized

Photo by Jose Crespo

LISA COLBY

Spring Ring, 2003

3.2 x 2.2 x .6 cm

Sterling silver; hand constructed,

forged, oxidized

Photo by Steve Mann

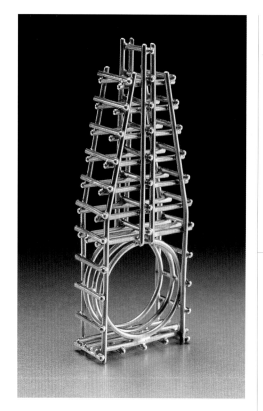

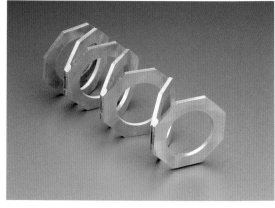

JULIE A. MATHEIS

Recurrence, 2001

2.5 x 2.5 x 16 cm (extended)

Sterling silver; fabricated

Photo by Marty Doyle

BEN NEUBAUER

Spire Ring, 2003

5 x 1.9 x .9 cm

18-karat palladium

white gold; fabricated

Courtesy of Mobilia Gallery,

Cambridge, Massachusetts

Photo by Courtney Frisse

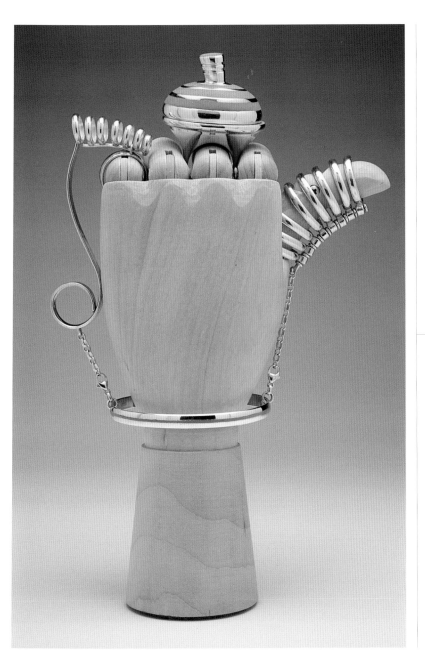

YUKA SAITO

Teapot, 2002
8.5 x 3 x 1 cm (handle);
5 x 3 x 2.3 cm (lid);
6 x 2.3 x 2.3 cm (spout)
Sterling silver, copper,
brass, resin
Courtesy of Mobilia Gallery,
Cambridge, Massachusetts
Photo by Robert Diamante

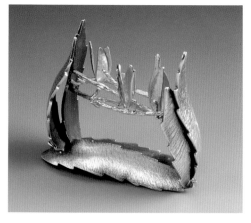

MI-SOOK HUR

Measuring Spoon Ring No. 2, 2003

6.9 x 5.4 x 5 cm

Sterling silver

Photo by artist

HELEN SHIRK

Two Finger Ring, 2003

4.4 x 5 x 1.9 cm

Silver, 18-karat gold; fabricated

Photo by artist

JUNGHYUN WOO

Something Sweet, 2001

5.4 x 5 x 5.2 cm (box)

Sterling silver, 18-karat gold;

die formed, etched, fabricated

Photos by Helen Shirk

MÓNICA SUÑER

My Little Monsters: Series I, 1999

5 x 2.5 cm (each)

Plastic scouring pads;

heat modeled

Photo by Petra Jaschke

● The interplay of light, color, and shape stimulate my artistic and creative nature. I endeavor to create a vivid color palette that offers viewers joyous and playful imagery. What powers will you have when you wear this work?

Nadine Fenton

NADINE FENTON

Ring for Movement: Purple & Yellow, 2001

12 x 2 x 2 cm

Artistic wire; crocheted, knitted

Photo by Claude-Simon Longlois

LORI A. MESSENGER

Cellular Banquet, 2002

3.8 x 3.2 x 3.2 cm

Soda-lime glass, sterling silver;

lampworked

Photo by artist

KAZ ROBERTSON

Swop Top Rings, 2002

1 x 1.5 x 1.5 cm to 1 x 3 x 3 cm

Silver, magnets, resin

Photo by John K. McGregor

PETRA BRENNER

Untitled, 2000

4 x 2.8 x 1.4 cm (average)

Colored glass, transparent glass,

precious stones; kiln cast

Photo by artist

CLAUDIO PINO

Prolifère Ring, 2003

3.8 x 3.2 x 1.9 cm

Sterling silver, 14-karat
gold, opal, emerald, ruby,
amethyst, moonstone, pearl
Photo by Philomène Longpré

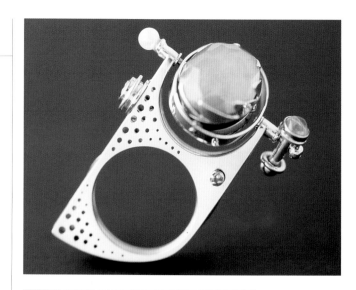

ANTON CEPKA

Ring, 1996

2 x 2 x 1.4 cm

Silver; cut, soldered

Photo by Slavomír Tomašovič

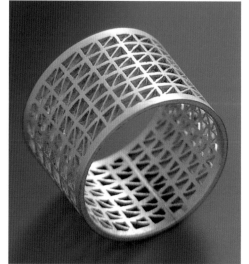

JACQUELYN CRISSMAN

Lethal Liana, 2002

20.3 x 8.9 x 8.9 cm

Sterling silver, fine silver, coral, iolite, brass
shavings, ostrich feathers, patina; fabricated,
cold forged, chased, repoussé, twining
Photos by Ericka Crissman (Wired Images)

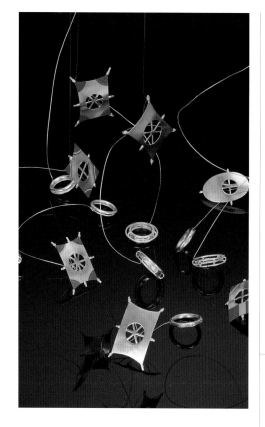

VRATISLAV KAREL NOVAK

Ring-Cube, 1995

25 x 18 x 25 cm

Stainless steel; soldered

Photo by Martin Tůma

JAY SONG

Kites (set of ten), 2002

Various dimensions

Sterling silver, gold foil,

oil paint; fabricated

Photo by Taweesak Molsawat

JEGAL WON

Three, Four, Five..., 2002

3 x 3.6 x 3.6 cm (each)

Sterling silver, wood, paint: fabricated

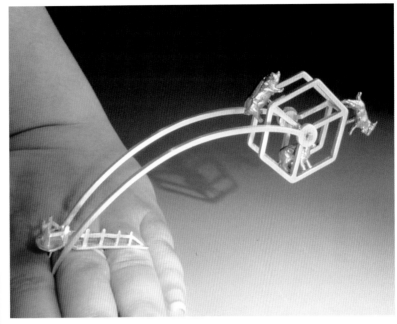

ALISON BRUNSON

Ferris Wheel Ring, 2001

10.7 x 8.9 x 1.9 cm

Sterling silver, gold plate; fabricated, cast

Photo by Dean Spencer

ANNE BAEZNER

Univers Clos (Closed Universe), 2001

8 x 4.5 x 2 cm

Silver, patinated silver

Photo by Maurice Aeschimann

FALKO MARX

Untitled, 1994

3.7 x 2.9 cm

Gold, platinum, ink, water,

porcelain miniature

Photo by Bernhard Schaub

KIM BUCK

Solitaire Ring, 2001

2 x 1.8 x 1 cm (left); 2 x 1.8 x .2 cm (center);

2 x 1.8 x .08 cm (right)

18-karat gold; machine-milled wax,

lost wax cast

Photo by Ole Akhøj

RUUDT PETERS

Ouroboros, Wunstorf, 1994

10.4 x 4 x 3.2 cm

Silver, marcasite, gold leaf

Photo by Rob Verscuys

SYLVIE PELLICER

Exterieur, 2002

1.5 cm high

Silver; hammered, riveted

Photo by Francis Coulon

MARIA PHILLIPS

Perpetual 3, 2003

3.8 x 5 x .6 cm

Enamel, steel cloisonné wire,

sterling silver; fabricated

Photo by Douglas Yaple

HANNE BEHRENS

Band Rings, 2001

2.4 x 2.4 x .9 cm (each)

18-karat white gold, 18-karat

yellow gold, 18-karat red gold;

woven, soldered, curved

Photo by artist

KATE CATHEY

Growth Ring, 2003

8.2 x 3.8 x .9 cm

Fine silver, enamel; die formed,

hollow constructed

Photo by Robert Diamante

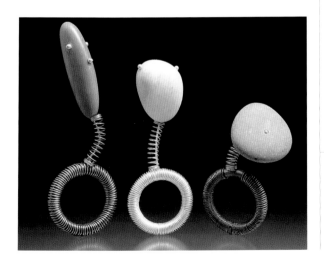

ANYA PINCHUK

Pebble Rings, 2000

7.6 x 2.5 x .9 cm (each)

Sterling silver, steel springs,

pebbles; fabricated

Photo by artist

REGINE SCHWARZER

Two Fingerring, 2002

3.2 x 4.1 x 2.1 cm

Sterling silver, 22-karat gold,

mabe pearl, prehnite, chrysoprase

Photo by Grant Hancock

ROBERT W. EBENDORF

Collection of 16 Rings, 1995

Various dimensions

Iron, 18-karat gold, beach glass, copper,

silver, mixed media; constructed

Photo by James Milmoe

DEE FONTANS

Hand Piece, 1998

3.2 x 3.8 x 3.8 cm

Sterling silver, 24-karat gold, chrysoprase,

garnet, citrine; cuttlefish cast, hollow

constructed, soldered, bezel set

Photo by Charles Lewton-Brain

PETER CHANG

Ring, 2003

5.6 x 5 x 2.5 cm

Acrylic, resin, silver, gold; carved, laminated

Photo by artist

JASON PENN

AZ River Stone, 2002

3 x 2.6 x .9 cm

Found Arizona river stone,
18-karat gold tube, Arizona anthill
garnet; carved, drilled, rivet set

Photo by Azad

DEBORAH LOZIER

Untitled, 2001
3.5 x 3.3 x .8 cm (center)
3.3 x 3.3 x 1 cm (below);
Copper, enamel; fold formed,
anticlastic raised, torch fired
Photos by Hap Sakwa

In this series of rings, I encouraged the claylike qualities of copper by using a relaxed approach with the hammer and enhanced this illusion with a torch fired enamel "glaze." Each ring is large yet comfortable, leaving a memory of its presence well after it is removed.

Deborah Lozier

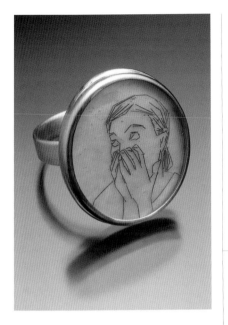

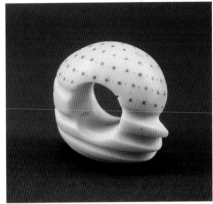

The wonder and the mystery of what is under the brown tagua nut skin fascinates me. Once uncovered, the real magic begins. By removal processes, I strive to create and discover a worthy three-dimensional art form.

David LaPlantz

DAVID LaPLANTZ

Red Dots Duck, 2002

4.4 x 4.2 x 2 cm

Tagua nut; constructed, fabricated

Photo by artist

MELANIE BILENKER

Observer, 2003

2.3 x 2 x 2.4 cm

18-karat gold, ivory-piano-key

laminate, epoxy resin, hair

strands, watch crystal

Photo by Ken Yanoviak

DOROTHY HOGG MBE

Ring of Rings, 1994

2.2 x 2.2 x 2.2 cm

Silver, 18-karat gold

Photo by John K. McGregor

SUSAN MYERS

Triumph, 2000

5 x 3.8 x .9 cm

Sterling silver, 24-karat gold plate,

tanzanite, black pearl

Photo by Douglas Yaple

HAROLD O'CONNOR

Table Top Ring, 2001

3 x 2 x 2.7 cm

Silver, fine gold, 18-karat gold, sugulite;

fabricated, roller printed

Photo by artist

JANE BALFOUR

Rail Ring, 2001

2.3 x .4 x .3 cm

Platinum, 18-karat yellow gold,

diamonds, sapphires

Photo by Chris Reeve Photography

The important parts of this ring are the vases and the number three. In the Korean culture these symbols mean good luck. (You can put three fingers in the center ring at the same time.)

Hea-Rim Shin

HEA-RIM SHIN

Prayer, 2002

Various dimensions

Sterling silver, wood, gold plate, patina;

fabricated, kum-boo

Photo by Kwang-Chun Park (KC Studio)

ALEXANDRA de SERPA PIMENTEL

Untitled, 2000

4.3 x 3.4 x 3.1 cm

Sterling silver, 19-karat gold; fabricated

Photo by artist

BRUCE METCALF

Wide Red Ring, 2003

5 x 6.4 x 2.5 cm

Gold-plated silver, wood;

cast, carved, painted

Photo by artist

BENITA EDWARDS

Pearl Ring, 2002

2.2 x 1.9 x .4 cm

9-karat yellow gold, pink sapphires,

pink freshwater pearl

Photo by artist

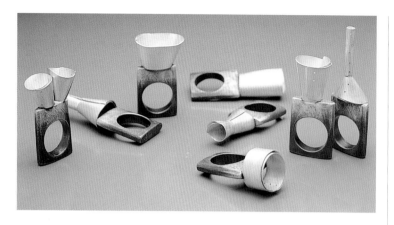

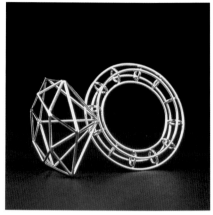

YEUN HEE RYU

Vessels, 2002

2 x 4.5 x 1 cm (average)

Sterling silver

Photo by Myung-Wook Huh (Studio Munch)

GREG SIMS

Diamond Ring–Wire Frame, 2003

4 x 2.5 x 2.5 cm

18-karat gold, platinum wire;

laser welded

Photo by artist

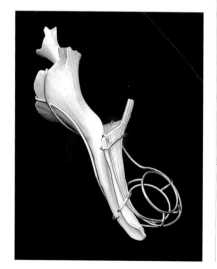

SHINGO FURUKAWA

Ring with a Shell, 2003

8.9 x 12 x 4.4 cm

Sterling silver, seashell

Photo by Chuck Pappas

(Third Eye Photography)

DANIELA HOFFMANN

Generations Rings:
Rose, Camellia (2), Ellipse, 2000
3 x 4 x 2 cm (each)
Sterling silver, 18-karat yellow
gold, diamonds, patina; hand
fabricated, constructed
Photos by Hap Sakwa

CHRISTINE DHEIN

Cage Ring, 2002

2.5 x 2.2 x 2.2 cm

18-karat gold, diamonds, rubber;

hand fabricated

Photo by George Post

PAVEL HERYNEK

Homage to My Mother, 2003

8 x 8.5 x 8.9 cm

Plastic

Courtesy of Galerie V & V,

Vienna, Austria

Photo by Markéta Ondrusková

G. McLARTY

Ring 7032, 2003

9.5 x 8.5 x 3.8 cm

Copper, cement, enamel,
collage, mica, 24-karat gold leaf

Photo by Jack Zilker

SHIMON KAHLOUN

Ebony Rings, 2001

3 x 3.5 cm (average)

Ebony, crushed turquoise,
silver; hand carved, inlaid

Photo by Miguel Torres

CLAUDIA RINNEBERG

Spirit of Elements, 2003

4.2 x 3.8 x 2 cm

Iron, 14-karat gold; sawed, bent

Photo by Federico Cavicchioli

JONATHAN WAHL

Rings, 2002

2.7 x 2.4 x 1.2 cm (left);

2.6 x 2.4 x 1.3 cm (right)

Mild steel, gold solder; patterned, inlaid

Photo by Bob Barrett

ANNA RAIGORODSKAIA

Kidnapping, 2000

3.5 x 1.8 x 3 cm

Silver; cast, hand

fabricated, oxidized

Photo by Alexander Ivanov

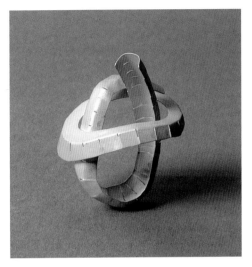

NORMAN WEBER

Untitled, 1993

4.7 x 4.1 x 3.4 cm

8-karat gold; soldered

Photo by artist

TOM McCARTHY

Jan Ring, 2003

2.5 x 2.1 x 2.1 cm

Sterling silver, cement, steel,

cubic zirconia; fabricated

Photo by artist

TIMOTHY LAZURE

Untitled, 2003

3.4 x 2.3 x 2.1 cm

Sterling silver, 14-karat gold,

beach pebble, ruby

Photos by artist

JASON MORRISSEY

Aquatic Rings, 2003

3.2 x 3.2 x 3.2 cm (left and right); 3.2 x 3.8 x 3.8 cm (center)

Sterling silver, borosilicate glass cabochons;

cuttlefish cast, blown

Photo by Robert Diamante

PAZ FERNÁNDEZ

Femme Couture, 2001

3.8 x 4.4 x 4.4 cm

Sterling silver, 18-karat gold,
22-karat gold, topaz,
diamonds, pearls, rubber sole;
fabricated, granulated

Photo by Peter Groesbeck

REBECCA SCHEER

Forged and Pierced Rings, 1999–2001

1.9 x 2.5 x 2.5 cm (largest)

Sterling silver, fine silver, 14-karat gold;
forged, pierced

Photo by artist

HEATHER WHITE

Circle Ring: Halo, 2002

4.4 x 3.8 x 2.2 cm

Gold, steel, pearls; constructed

Photo by Dean Powell

INGJERD HANEVOLD

Flowering, 2003

7 x 3.5 cm

Bronze, patina, lacquer

Photo by artist

MARIANNE SCHLIWINSKI

OXX, 2002

6.1 x 3.5 x .7 cm

Fine silver, tin; printed, constructed

Photos by Jürgen Eickhoff

KIMIAKI KAGEYAMA

Suzushita, 2002

4.5 x 2.5 x 3.5 cm

Urushi (Japanese lacquer), resin,

mineral pigments, gold pigments,

18-karat yellow gold

Photo by artist

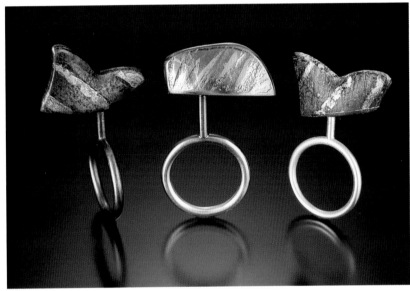

JOSÉE DESJARDINS

To Understand All in a Single Life, 1999

6 x 5 x 2.8 cm

Sterling silver, enamel, ancient

glass, siliconized tile grout;

lost wax cast, mosaic

Photo by Paul Simon

ADRIENNE M. GRAFTON-KANAZAWA

Mountains, 2003

4.5 x 3 x .5 cm (each)

Sterling silver, copper, 24-karat gold;

die formed, kum-boo, kum-pak

Photo by Robert Diamante

DAVID HENSEL

Opening Rings, 1978

11 x 9 x 9 cm (left, open);

10 x 10 x 10 cm (right, open)

Wood, ivory, silver, gold; carved,

hinged, constructed

Photo by Barbara Cartlidge

KEITH A. LEWIS

XY:XY Ring, 2002

2.5 x 3 x 3 cm

Sterling silver, 18-karat gold,

graphite, enamel

Photos by artist

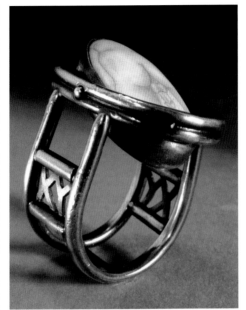
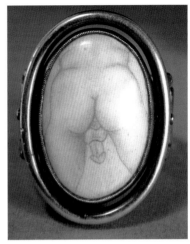

INGJERD HANEVOLD

Collector's Ring, 2001

6 x 4.5 cm

Oxidized silver, seeds, cork

Photo by artist

313

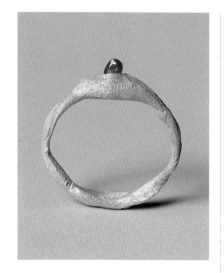

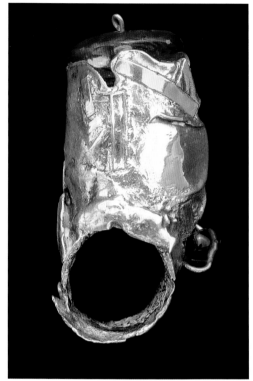

KARL FRITSCH

Ruby Ring I, 2002

3 x 2 x 1 cm

Gold, ruby; cast

Photo by artist

EDNA KUHTA

Ring, 2001

6.4 x 3 x 2.5 cm

Sterling silver, gold, Baltic amber;

fused, rolled, textured

Photo by Chris Kuhta

LOUISE NORRELL

Garnet Ring, 2002

2.5 x 1.7 x 2 cm

18-karat yellow gold, 18-karat
white gold, garnet; forged,
chased, soldered, bezel set
Photo by Walker Montgomery

GINA PANKOWSKI

Verve, 2002

6.9 x 1.3 x 1.3 cm

18-karat gold, yellow sapphires,
blue sapphires; cast, fabricated
Photo by Douglas Yaple

JACQUELINE RYAN

Untitled, 2001

2.5 x 2 x 2 cm

18-karat gold, enamel;

pierced, constructed

Photo by Giovanni Corvaja

CHRISTA LÜHTJE

Ring, 2002

2.3 x 1.3 cm

22-karat gold; forged

Photo by Eva Jünger

GEOFFREY D. GILES

Pivotal Spinner, 2003

2.5 x .9 x .9 cm

18-karat yellow gold, diamonds;

fabricated, soldered, flush set

Photos by Taylor Dabney

MAH RANA

His 'n Hers, 1995–2002

6.5 x 2.1 cm

Gold (two used wedding bands)

Photo by George Meister

DANIEL KRUGER

Untitled, 2003

1.5 x 2.5 x 5 cm

18-karat gold, coral,
pearl; constructed

Photo by Thilo Haertlein

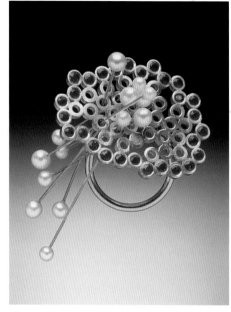

MIA MALJOJOKI

Cluster Series #1, 2003

2.5 x 2.5 x 2.5 cm

18-karat gold, silver, ruby, pearl

Photo by Dean Powell

By making jewelry, I study the relationships and diversity found when merging the same components in a variety of ways. Through my work, I contrast and inevitably compare properties of metal; processes of construction; movement of parts; ways that components are connected; textures; and colors. I create systems of opposites within opposites on several scales to generate rich complexity through simple binary. For inspiration manifesting these concepts into objects, I look to both the forms and movements found in the ocean and the violent life-giving forces of volcanoes.

Mia Maljojoki

⬤ **Kinetic motion is an important characteristic in my work. It keeps the pieces fresh and the wearer involved.**

Kristina S. Kada

KRISTINA S. KADA

Large Circle Ring, 1999

3.2 x 2.5 x 2.5 cm

Sterling silver, 22-karat gold
and sterling silver bimetal,
tanzanites; hand fabricated

Photo by Hap Sakwa

LYDIA V. GERBIG-FAST

X Ring, 2001

2.5 x 2.5 x 2.5 cm

Pearl, uncut diamond, sterling silver,
14-karat yellow gold, 18-karat yellow
gold; fabricated

Photo by artist

PAUL PRESTON

Carved Pebble Stoat, 1983

2.6 cm high

Cornish beach pebble
(black slate), fine gold;
carborundum wheel carved

Photo by Chris Bowerman

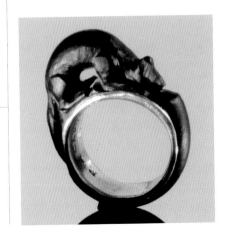

SASKIA BOSTELMANN

I Got You Wrapped Around My Finger...A Love Story, 2001–2003

3 x 2.5 x 2 cm (average)

Sterling silver, 18-karat yellow gold; wax carved, cast

Photo by Enrique Bostelmann

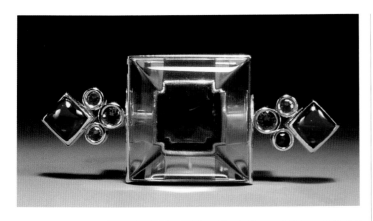

CHRIS KUHTA

Gold & Silver Ring, 2000

2.8 x 2.8 x .5 cm

Sterling silver, gold;

coaxial constructed

Photos by artist

LING HE

Magnificat: Theotokos II, 2002

Variable dimensions

Sterling silver, rock crystal,

corundum, cubic zirconia

Photos by artist

YuCHUN CHEN

Untitled, 2001

4.5 x 2.5 x 1.8 cm

Sterling silver, red pom-pom

Photos by Federico Cavicchioli

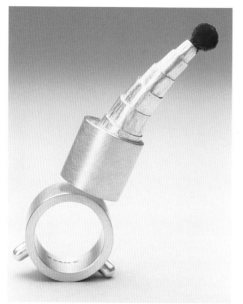

JOANA KAO

Seven-Year Itch, 2003

7.6 x 2.2 x 1.3 cm

Sterling silver, copper,

18-karat gold; fabricated

Photo by James Chan

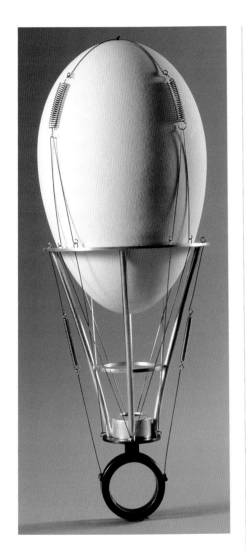

CECE WIRE

Tower Road Silos, 2002

4.4 x 5 x 1.9 cm

Fine silver, sterling silver;

soldered, constructed

Photo by Kyle Castle

SIGURD BRONGER

Ring, 1999

12 x 4 cm

Steel, silver, goose egg shell

Photo by artist

RIE TANIGUCHI

Blue Antroll Ring/Box, 2003

3.5 x 2 x 5 cm

Sterling silver, iolite, enamel,

9-karat gold; press formed,

soldered, riveted, pegged, cast

Photo by Joël Degen

● The Greek god Hermes inspired this ring. Hermes, who is traditionally known as the god of commerce or the messenger god, was, amongst other things, a master thief. This unusual verity is what motivated me to create this ring, a thief's ring.

Kirk Lang

KIRK LANG

Mercurius, 2002

3.2 x 3.8 x 1.3 cm

Sterling silver, optic lens, meteorite

Photo by Mike Cirelli

● I like the chal-
lenge of dealing
with wearability.
All my pieces are
extremely wear-
able even if, at
first glance, they
look as though
they may not be.
I enjoy the surprise
when the wearer
finds out their
fingers fit the
ring's geometry.

Dorothy Hogg MBE

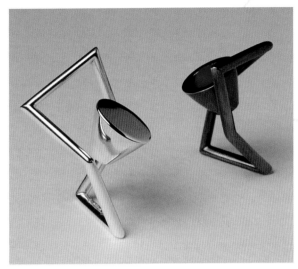

DOROTHY HOGG MBE

Walking Rings, 2002–2003

4 x 2 x 2 cm

Silver, oxidized silver, red fleece

Photo by John K. McGregor

JOON HEE KIM

Fly I, 2003

5 x 6 x 2 cm

Sterling silver

Photo by Myung-Wook Huh

(Studio Munch)

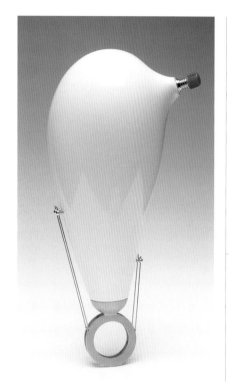

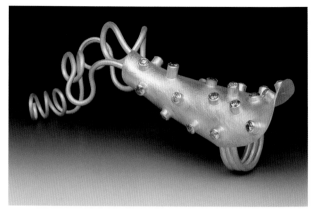

SO YOUNG PARK

Vitality, 2003

8.9 x 3.8 x 3.8 cm

Sterling silver, cubic zirconia

Photo by Dan Neuberger

SIGURD BRONGER

Ring, 1996

13 x 3 cm

Steel, silver, hard foam, lacquer

Photo by artist

This piece was inspired by an article entitled "The Good Wife's Guide" published by *Housekeeping Monthly* in 1955. Each featured product was meant to assist a wife in her daily chores. The *Finger Dusters* allow a wife to clean in hard-to-reach places and still have the use of her hands to pick up items such as toys and clothes.

Meredith Anne Sutton

ULO FLORACK

Duck Tail Missing, 2001

3 x 2 x 3 cm

Silver, enamel; lost wax cast

Photo by artist

MEREDITH ANNE SUTTON

Finger Dusters, 2003

3.8 x 3.8 cm (each)

Sterling silver, feathers;

hand dyed, fabricated

Photo by Campus Photography,

Savannah College of Art and Design

YEONKYUNG KIM

Socksrings, 2003

3.4 x 3.4 x 1.9 cm

Socks; folded

Photo by artist

KRISTIN MITSU SHIGA

Happy Trails (Ring for Brad), 2003

3.8 x 2.5 x 2.5 cm

Sterling silver, steel, brass,

found object; cast, fabricated

Photo by Courtney Frisse

MARGERY F. COOPER

Standard Prong Setting, 2003

6.4 x 2.5 x 1.9 cm

Electric utility plug, sterling silver,

yellow quartz; bezel set, fabricated

Photo by artist

ALISON BRUNSON

Boat Ring, 2002

16.5 x 6.4 x 4.4 cm

Sterling silver, gold plate, resin;

cast, fabricated

Photo by Dean Spencer

BETH PIVER and
ANDY VICK

Assorted Rings, 1995–2003
1.3 x 1.9 x 1.9 cm (each)
Silver, copper, bronze,
brass, steel, stones;
riveted, cold connected
Photo by artists

HSIA-MAN LYDIA WANG

Untitled, 2002

5.4 x 5.4 x 2.2 cm

Sterling silver, coral; mokume gane,

fabricated

Photos by Jeffrey M. Bruce

NANCY MOYER

3 Degrees of Separation Ring, 2002

5 x 2.5 x 2.5 cm

Sterling silver, copper tubing, polishing

wheel, separation disks; married metals,

fabricated, soldered, formed

Photo by Robert Diamante

GEORG SPRENG

Ice Cream Cone Ring, 2003

6 x 4 x 4 cm

18-karat yellow gold, South Sea and

Akoya cultured pearls; hand constructed

Photo by Viscom Studios

I work with metal in much the same way as a jazz musician improvises on a melody.

Susan May

SUSAN MAY

Ring, 1999

4.5 x 4 x 3 cm

Sterling silver, 18-karat gold; forged

Photo by Joël Degen

ALICIA BOSWELL

Shayla's Memory, 2003

5 x 3.8 x 3.8 cm

Sterling silver, fine silver, enamel;
fabricated, crocheted

Photo by Peter Nassoit

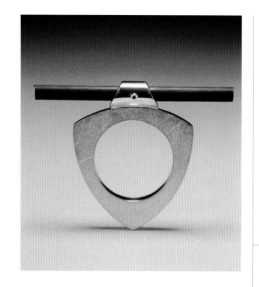

MARIE PLATTEAU-CLANCY

Untitled, 2001

10.2 x 4.4 x 4.4 cm

Sterling silver wire; crocheted

Photo by Jeffrey Clancy

BORIS BALLY

Triangle with Bar, 1992

3.2 x 3.8 x .5 cm

Sterling silver,

duranodized aluminum rod;

fabricated, cast, riveted

Photo by artist

My work represents ornaments of unusual proportions that shed a new light on the body. They announce themselves with a certain self-confidence, commenting on the sensuality of the skin and its movements. My goal is to produce designs that are innocent and attractive, but are also ambiguous and cause tension. I work with fluid organic geometries to reinforce the links between open or closed forms, creating internal spaces. With those forms I hope to invite the viewer to touch and to wear them.

Marie Platteau-Clancy

SABINE AMTSBERG

Untitled, 2001

2.7 x 3.6 x 1.4 cm

Sterling silver, gold plate, bone;

forged, engraved

Photo by Christoph Papsch

DIANNE M. REILLY

Ring, 2003

3.5 x 2.9 x 2.9 cm

Fine silver, enamel, gold ingot;

raised, rolled, drawn, fabricated,

soldered, prong set

Photo by artist

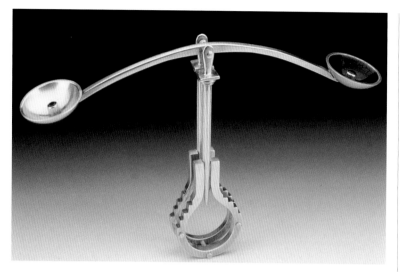

DANIELLE CRISSMAN

Lining the Pockets of Justice, 1999

12 x 7.6 x 1.9 cm

Silver, garnet, leaded enamel; fabricated,

riveted, hand engraved, carved

Photo by Jerry Anthony

J. E. PATERAK

Two Poddish Rings, 2001

3.2 x 3.8 cm (average)

Oxidized sterling silver, 22-karat gold,

24-karat gold, pearls; constructed

Photo by Robert Diamante

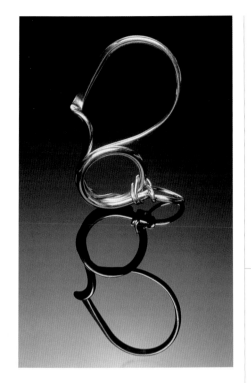

CAROLINE GORE

In, Within, or Out Series, 2003

1.5 x 2.2 x 2 cm (each)

24-karat gold, 14-karat gold, sterling

silver, ruby, citrine; kum-boo

Photo by artist

JIM COHEN

Carnival Ring, 2001

5 x .9 x .9 cm

18-karat yellow gold; forged

Photo by Jim Wildeman

MICHAL BAR-ON

Marriage #1, 1998

7 x 3.5 x .01 cm

22-karat gold, 24-karat gold foil;

hand cut, mill rolled, die formed

Photo by Shmaya Cohen

KENT RAIBLE

Temple Ring, 1998

3.5 x 2.5 x 2.5 cm

18-karat yellow gold, holly agate,

rubies; fabricated, granulated

Photo by Hap Sakwa

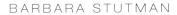

GIOVANNI CORVAJA

Untitled, 2000

2.2 x 1.2 x 2.2 cm

Fine wire; assembled

Photo by artist

BARBARA STUTMAN

A Show of Her Hand, 1995

8 x 2 x 1.7 cm

24-karat gold leaf, fine silver, sterling
silver, plastic; spool knitted, wrapped

Photo by Pierre Fauteux

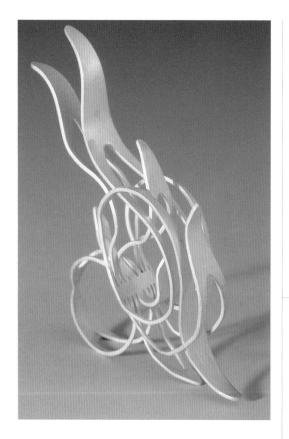

LUCY JADE SYLVESTER

Time Flies, 2000

4 x 3.5 x .6 cm

Gold, dandelion seeds, resin

Photo by Elly Crook

THOMAS J. LECHTENBERG

Folded Ring, 2002

4.4 x 7.6 x .9 cm

Sterling silver; fabricated

Photo by artist

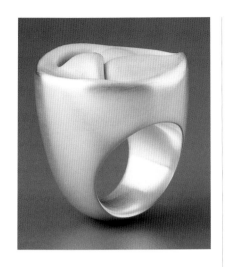

YUYEN CHANG

Orifice Series, 2003

2.5 x 2.5 x 3.2 cm

Fine silver, sterling silver

Photo by Jamie Young

INNI PÄRNÄNEN

Ring, 2003

3.2 x 3.8 x 3.8 cm

Sterling silver; etched, soldered

Photo by artist

● I am a thrift-store, garage-sale, flea-market hound. I love the thought of taking the old to create the new. What was once discarded and considered useless is now made into someone else's treasure. I try to let each piece dictate its new design, allowing it to be integrated fully into a new form of existence.

Shava Lawson

HERMAN HERMSEN

Crystalrock Ring, 1989

5 x 4 cm

Crystal

Photo by Tom Haartsent

SHAVA LAWSON

Rose Cocktail Ring, 2003

3.8 x 3.2 x 3.2 cm

Found cast acrylic button, sterling silver; fabricated

Photo by Douglas Yaple

PETER DECKERS

10 Most Wanted, 2000

3.2 x 1.7 x 2.5 cm

Sterling silver, crystal glass, digital prints; fabricated

Photo by artist

JIRO KAMATA

Tesa Rings, 2000
1.5 x 2.5 x 2.5 cm (each)
Silver, fine gold plate,
tape, lipstick print
Photos by artist

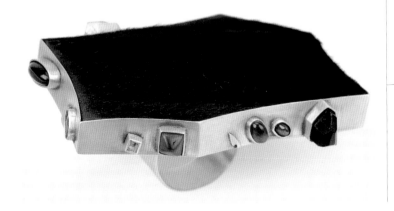

KADRI MÄLK

Hunting Field, 1999
4.5 x 6 x 2.7 cm
Silver, moleskin, rubber, indigolite,
verdelite, tourmaline, hematite,
amethyst, shark's tooth, emerald
Photo by Tiit Rammul

343

TOD PARDON

Nibble Ring, 2003

6.4 x 3.2 x .6 cm

Sterling silver, 14-karat yellow gold, wood, bone, pigment, glass, pearls, hematite; fabricated, inlaid

Photo by Stock Studios Photography

● Featuring humorous, brightly colored, figurative pieces, my work deals with the duality of the human condition and its inherent anxiety. As the Indian poet Rabindranath Tagore said, "Truth in her dress finds facts too tight. In fiction she moves with ease."

Tod Pardon

MIRIAM VERBEEK

Silence, 1997

4 x 2.5 x .6 cm

Crystal, beeswax, cotton

Photo by Hennie van Beek

SOFIA CALDERWOOD

Contact, 2002

3.8 x 5 x 5 cm

Sterling silver, patina, foam earplugs

Photo by artist

ROBERT DANCIK

Ring Finger, Finger Ring, 2003

3.2 x 2.5 x 3.2 cm

Sterling silver, 18-karat gold,

precious metal clay, nail polish;

press molded, fabricated

Photo by Ralph Gabriner

⬤ **Altering and exaggerating natural shapes, especially plant forms, has an important role in my work. I like to reflect the inspirational, the hopeful, and the majestic qualities of life.**

So Young Park

SO YOUNG PARK

Sprouting I, 2003

8.9 x 15.2 x 8.9 cm

Sterling silver, sapphire, ruby

Photo by Ga Rim Hong

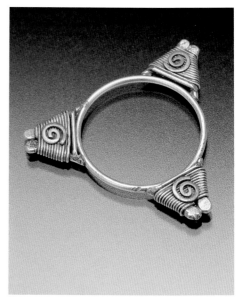

CHUCK DOMITROVICH

Untitled, 1995

3.2 cm in diameter

Sterling silver, fine silver, 14-karat gold

Photo by Douglas Yaple

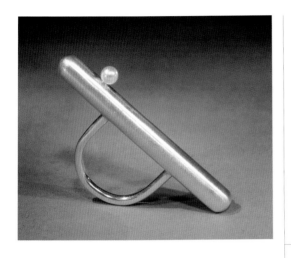

SHIN LYOUNG KIM

Ja..., 2002
Various dimensions
Stainless steel ruler, sterling silver

DEVON CLARK

Bare, 2000
3 x 5 x .5 cm
Sterling silver, pearl
Photo by Geri Solodky

AI MORITA

*Ring with Four Interchangeable
Centers and Eight Pins II*, 2003
2.5 x 5.2 x 5.2 cm (assembled)
Silver, gold plate, gold leaf, mother-of-
pearl pins; inlaid, oxidized, mounted
Photo by artist

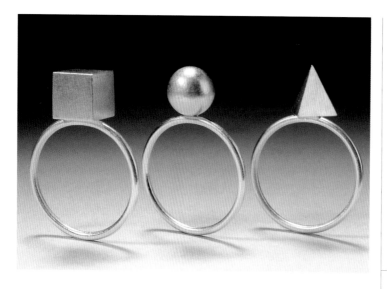

KARI WOO

Temple Ring, 2002

3.2 x 3.2 x 3.2 cm

Sterling silver, 10-karat gold,

found rusted washer,

turquoise, diamond; fabricated

Photo by artist

LAUREN LaPIERRE

Geometrings, 2000

2.5 x 1.9 x .7 cm (each)

Sterling silver; hollow

formed, fabricated

Photo by Mark Johnston

ANTJE ILLNER

Flying, 2002
4 x 2 x 1 cm
Glass disks, sterling silver;
slumped, set, soldered
Photo by Amanda Mansell

PATTY L. COKUS

Articulated Frusta: Ring #1, 2001
2.8 x 2.5 x 1.6 cm (collapsed)
Sterling silver; fabricated,
hollow constructed
Photo by Douglas Yaple

NOVA SAMODAI

Ball Bearing Series: Ring 3.14 mm, 1999

3 x 3 x 1.3 cm

Sterling silver, copper, stainless steel

ball bearings

Photo by Dean Powell

SHANA ASTRACHAN

Black Felted Ring, 2003

2.5 x 1.6 x .3 cm

18-karat gold, oxidized sterling

silver, silk, mohair; knotted,

wrapped, felted

Photo by Chris McCaw

KIM JONES

Emerging, 2001

1.9 x 1.9 x 1.9 cm

22-karat gold, oxidized

sterling silver; fabricated

Photo by Ralph Gabriner

KIRBY W. McELROY

Washer Ring, 2002

2.5 x 2.5 x .3 cm

Steel washer, 18-karat gold, sterling silver;

bezel set, backed, wrapped

Photo by David Ramsey

● I intuitively construct from an initial two-dimensional line drawing, continually reassessing and refining the form as I make the piece. Spatial relations, contrast and complexity, fine details and shadows are carefully considered. I have been dominantly using gold and mild steel. I am attracted to gold for being soft, having a rich color, and conveying a sense of purity.

Mari Funaki

MARI FUNAKI

Rings, 2000

2.8 x 2.8 x 1.5 cm (largest)

22-karat gold; fabricated

Photo by Terence Borgue

WILLIAM RICHEY

Untitled, 2002

3.8 x 2.5 cm

Platinum, 18-karat yellow gold, diamonds; cast, fabricated

Photo by Robert Diamante

JANA BREVICK

The Everchanging Ring, 1999

2.5 x .5 cm

24-karat gold; forged, chased

Photo by Douglas Yaple

ERICO NAGAI

Tube 3, 1996

3.2 x 2.6 x 1.3 cm

28-karat gold, aquamarine,

Mexican fire opal

Photos by George Meister

JACLYN DAVIDSON

Alien Ring, 1999

3.2 x 2.5 x .6 cm

18-karat gold, diamonds; hand
fabricated, wax carved, cast,
filed, chased, engraved, set

Photo by Ralph Gabriner

MARIA PACE PELLEGRINI

Cucú, 2003

3.4 x 2.8 x .5 cm

18-karat gold, 22-karat gold,
emerald, fire opal; constructed

Photo by Federico Cavicchioli

HELENA ANDERSSON

Wedding Ring, 1999

3.9 x 2.3 x 1.1 cm

18-karat gold plate, sterling silver,

garnet bead, sapphire bead,

emerald bead

Photo by artist

EILEEN GERSTEIN

Woven Wedding Set, 2003

.6 x 2.5 cm (left);

1.3 x 2.2 cm (right)

22-karat gold wire; textured,

intertwined, fabricated

Photo by Hap Sakwa

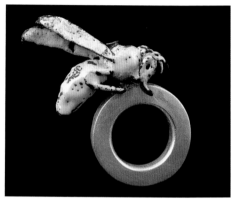

Bee Ring, 2002

3.8 x 4.4 x .9 cm

Copper, enamel, silver;
electroformed, cast

Photo by Brantley Carrol

ROBERT LONGYEAR

Abstracted Purity, 2002

2.5 x 2.5 x 2.5 cm (each)

Sterling silver, enamel; water cast,
torch fired, fabricated

Photo by Don Casper

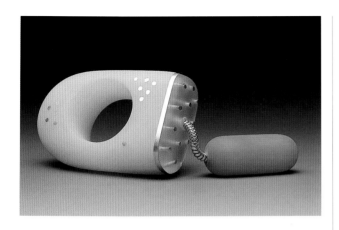

SARAH CRAWFORD

Twizzley, 2003

5.5 x 2.2 x .8 cm

Nylon, sterling silver;

constructed, joined

Photo by R. Strout

BRAD WINTER

White Ring, 2000

2.2 x 3.8 x 1 cm

Steel, white paint, red grout

Photo by Tom Mills

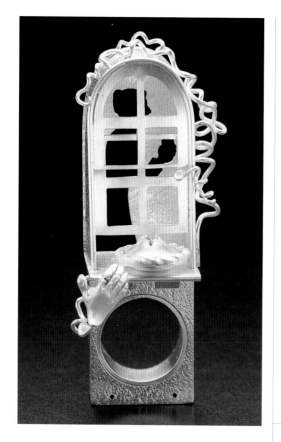

PAMELA MORRIS THOMFORD

Sneaky Pete, 2001

7.6 x 3.2 x 2.5 cm

Sterling silver, precious metal clay, fine silver;

roller printed, cast, fired, fabricated

Photo by Keith Meiser

THOMAS MANN

4 Rings, from the *Found Object*

Container Series, 2003

Various dimensions

Silver, bronze, iron, acrylic, flourescent acrylic,

shredded money, found objects; fabricated

Photo by Will Crocker

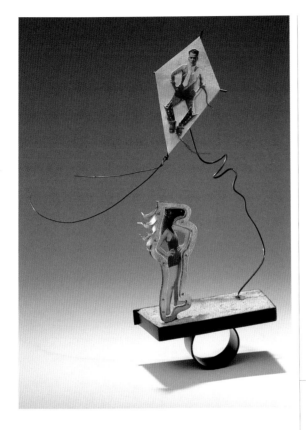

G. McLARTY

Ring 7031, 2003

15.9 x 10.8 x 3.2 cm

Copper, cement, collage, mica,

antique book paper, thread,

24-karat gold leaf

Photo by Jack Zilker

IRIS EICHENBERG

Untitled, 1998

4 x 4.5 x 1.5 cm

Silver, porcelain,

medical foam; cast

Photo by Ron Zijlstia

359

My mother kept an amazing collapsible plastic cup in her purse that transformed from a flat object into a container able to hold a refreshing drink. The cup's ability to expand and collapse was due to its assembly of *frusta*—truncated cones—nestled into each other but capped at the narrow end to prevent them from falling apart. The *Articulated Frusta* series is an exploration of this construction technique to produce multiple freely growing and receding wearable forms. The unimpeded movement and organization of these parts is what fascinates me. Each piece is ultimately dependent on the wearer to evoke or coax, with the slightest touch or movement, the various shapes and positions attainable. Subtle chinking reveals every shift.

Patty L. Cokus

PATTY L. COKUS

Articulated Frusta: Phonograph Ring, 2002

5 x 4.4 x 4.4 cm (extended);

3.8 x 3.8 x 4.4 cm (collapsed)

Sterling silver, black patina,

14-karat yellow gold; fabricated

Photos by artist

DAHLIA KANNER

4 Finger Ring, 2000

6 x 8.6 x 2.2 cm

Silver, patina; cast

Photo by Mark Johnston

YAYO

Puzzle 6, 2002

2 x 2 cm

Sterling silver; cast, oxidized

Photo by artist

PIA JILSØY

Betweenfingerring, 2002

3 x 6 x 3.3 cm

Aluminum, PVC, nylon, acrylic;

hand painted, laminated

Photo by artist

FELICITY PETERS

I Must Learn to Say — — !, 2002

4.5 x 2.2 x .4 cm

Sterling silver, 24-karat gold;

constructed, kum-boo

Photo by Victor France

FELIEKE van der LEEST

Party Goldfish in Pool, 2002

5 x 5 x 2.5 cm (ring without pool)

Viscose polyester/polyamide textile,

rubber fish, 18-karat gold; crocheted

Photo by Eddo Hartmann

MARY DONALD

Three Hundred Sixty-Five Days: A Journal, 2001–2002

1.9 x 1.9 x 1.9 cm (each)

Color photo transparencies, sterling silver

Photo by artist

RUUDT PETERS

Ouroboros, Mibladen, 1994

3 x 4 x 6 cm

Silver, desert rose, paint

Photo by Rob Verscuys

BARBARA TERRELL PUJOL

Empress Ring, 2002

2.2 x 1.1 x .5 cm

18-karat gold, diamond, amethyst

cabochons; forged, fabricated

Photo by Edward Sturr

MARIE CHAMBLIN DIROM

Pearl Ring, 1998

3 x 2.1 x 1.9 cm

Black South Sea pearl, orange sapphires,

18-karat yellow gold; fabricated, cast

Photo by Taylor Dabney

ROB JACKSON

Nail Ring, 2000

1.3 x 2.2 x 2.2 cm

100-year-old wrought iron nail,

found steel fragment, 18-karat gold,

20-karat gold, ruby; fabricated

Photo by artist

YONG JIN CHUNG

Geometric Rings, 2002

2.2 x 2.2 x .9 cm (each)

18-karat gold, diamonds; fabricated

Photo by Kwang-Chun Park

(KC Studio)

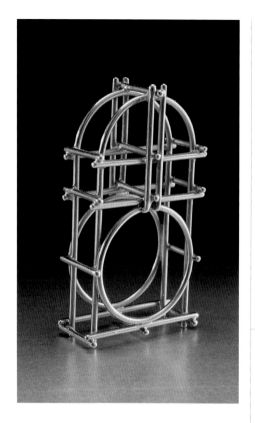

JACQUELINE RYAN

Untitled, 2001

3 x 4.4 x 4.8 cm

Gold; forged, pierced

Photo by Giovanni Corvaja

BEN NEUBAUER

Roman Arch Ring, 2002

3.8 x 1.9 x .9 cm

18-karat yellow gold; fabricated

Courtesy of Mobilia Gallery,

Cambridge, Massachusetts

Photo by Courtney Frisse

NANETTE M. JOLLY

A Ring for Ahn: Perpetuation, 2003

2.2 x 1.2 x .3 cm

Fine silver, sterling silver;

handwoven, fabricated

Photo by Gina Rymarcsuk

ARLINE M. FISCH

Tapered Spiral, 2001

7.6 x 3.8 x 3.8 cm

Sterling silver, nickel; spiral

braid construction

Photo by artist

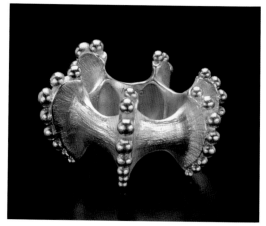

KRISTINA S. KADA

Cluster Ring, 2001

3.2 x 2.8 x 2.8 cm

Sterling silver; hand fabricated

Photo by Hap Sakwa

ALEXANDRA HART

Venus Ring, 2002

1.9 x 3.5 x 3.5 cm

Sterling silver, 18-karat gold;

wax carved, cast,

constructed, soldered

Photo by David Harrison

NANCY MUSTAPICH

Rose Quartz Ring, 2000

2.5 x 1.6 x 2.3 cm

Rose quartz, sterling silver;

fabricated

Photo by Bill Lemke

LORI MÜLLER

Cathedral Ring, 2003

4.8 x 2.2 x 1.5 cm

Sterling silver, citrine;

constructed, rivet set

Photo by Lauch McKenzie

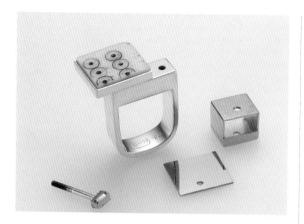

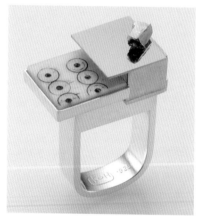

SHARON MASSEY

Adjustable Rings, 2002

5 x 1.3 x 1.9 cm (each)

Bronze, cubic zirconia;

fabricated, set

Photo by artist

HEE-SEUNG KOH

Piling-up 2, 2003

3.5 x 2.5 x 1.5 cm

Sterling silver, 24-karat gold,

18-karat gold, ivory, stainless steel

Photos by Kwang-Chun Park

(KC Studio)

MARIA BÖRJESSON

Architect's Rings, 2001

2 x 1.5 x 2 cm (each)

Black oxidized silver, silver, gold

Photo by Jan Ekblom

ELLEN CHEEK

Back to Basics, 1999

8.9 x 2.5 x 1.6 cm

Fine silver, sterling silver, 18-karat

gold, 9B drawing pencil; fabricated

Photo by Hap Sakwa

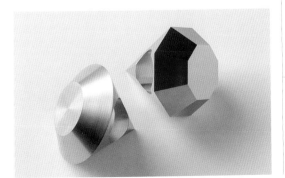

OTTO KÜNZLI

Solitaire (two rings), 1985

4 cm in diameter (left);

3.5 x 3.5 x 4.1 cm (right)

Stainless steel

Photo by artist

TIMOTHY LAZURE

Untitled, 2002

3.7 x 2.4 x 1.2 cm

Sterling silver, 14-karat gold;
die formed

Photo by artist

TAWEESAK MOLSAWAT

One, Two, Three...the Higher, the Colder, 2003

7.6 x 5.4 x 5.4 cm

Sterling silver, copper, brass, U.S. currency,
patina; cast, fabricated

Photo by artist

KARIN SEUFERT

Untitled, 2000

4.5 x 2.5 x 2.5 cm

Silver, glass beads, nylon

wire, silver crochet wire;

crocheted, embroidered

Photo by artist

MARY LEWIS

Whack-a-Mole Ring #2, 2002

3.8 x 1.3 x 1.3 cm

Sterling silver, stainless steel;

cast gears, hand fabricated

Photo by Dan Neuberger

TRACY STEEPY

Undie Ring Series, 2002

3.8 x 3.2 x 2.5 cm (largest)

Copper, acrylic urethane

Photo by Richard Gehrke

BRIDGET CATCHPOLE

From the series *Au Bonheur des Dames*

(To the Ladies' Happiness), 2002

3.8 x 2.5 x 2.5 cm

Sterling silver, freshwater pearls,

plastic; constructed

Photo by Paul Simon

Inspired by nineteenth-century kitsch and the Victorian popular interest in marine life and aquariums, I created this body of work. Resembling sea anemones and urchins, these pieces parody the shell-encrusted alcoves and parlors decorated by the middle- and upper-class women of the era. The work examines the notions of preciousness and fantasy, as well as the boredom and repression of Victorian upper-class women.

Bridget Catchpole

LOUISE PERRONE

Flower Power, 2003

4 x 3 x 3 cm

Anodized aluminum,

sterling silver; constructed

Photo by J. J. Mestinsek

KYUNG-HEE KIM

Episode of Ring III: Blossom in Silence, 2003

1.5 x 2.1 x 3 cm (each)

Sterling silver, gold leaf, jade, quartz,

carnelian; kum-boo

Photo by Myung-Wook Huh (Studio Munch)

DEBORAH BOSKIN

Urban Flora Rings, 2000

11.4 x 3.8 x 3.8 cm (each)

Copper, sterling silver, rock,

Prismacolor® pencils

Photo by Donald Felton

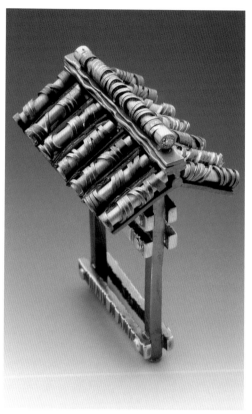

ROBERT LONGYEAR

Beats, Wisdom, and Blood, 2003

2.5 x 2.5 x 2.8 cm

10-karat gold, fine silver,

enamel, diamond

Photo by Don Casper

JENNIFER J. FECKER

Her Gate Is Always Open, 2001

4.4 x 2.5 x 1.6 cm

Sterling silver, 14-karat gold, Canadian

wild rice, diamonds; hand constructed

Photo by George Post

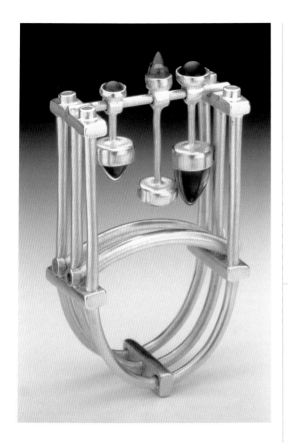

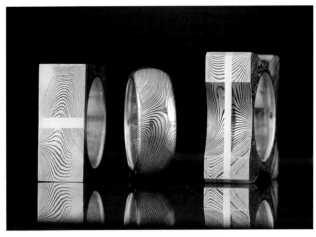

G. PHIL POIRIER

A Rose Between Two Thorns, 2003

2.4 x 2.4 x .9 cm (average)

Damascus stainless steel,

18-karat gold; inlaid

Photo by artist

I thrive on pushing the limits of any given material. In this example, the non-traditional and high-tech damascened stainless steel is blended with traditional 18-karat gold and formed into both time-honored and uniquely innovative shapes.

G. Phil Poirier

DANIELLE MILLER-GILLIAM

Nervous Habit Ring #6, 1996

4.4 x 2.5 x 1.3 cm

Sterling silver, citrine, peridot,

amethyst; hand fabricated

Photo by Peter Groesbeck

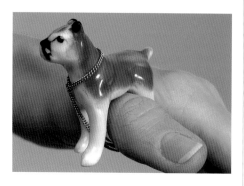

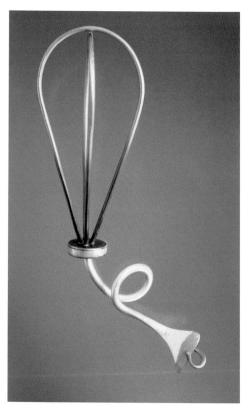

MECKY van den BRINK

Dog's Faith, 1994

6 x 5 x 2.5 cm

Porcelain, gold

Photos by Henni van Beek

SEAN DOYLE

Whisk It, 1999

15.2 x 7.6 x 6.4 cm

Sterling silver, nickel; fabricated

Photo by artist

ANDRÉE WEJSMANN

Watering Can, 2003

5 x 2.5 x 5.7 cm

Oxidized sterling silver; fabricated

Photo by artist

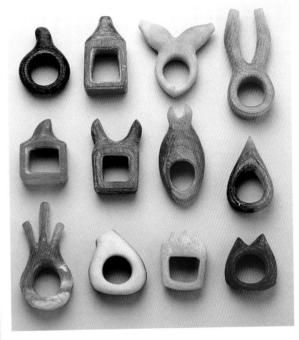

EUN-YOUNG MOON

Finding Mass, 2002

Various dimensions

Epoxy resin, pastel powder;

mixed, dried, carved

Photo by Myung-Wook Huh (Studio Munch)

This piece is my take on the work I feel I have to do to engage others in conversation. Worn in the palm of the hand (so as not to be forgotten) it is a daily reminder to take care and tend your relationships. It is a humorous piece about how awkward these efforts can often become.

Andrée Wejsmann

JEANETTE CALMETTE

Chess Series: Pawn, 2003
6.3 x 3.2 x 3.2 cm (on stand)
3.2 x 2.5 x 2.5 cm (right)
Sterling silver, brass found object;
hydraulically formed, fabricated
Photos by Eric Vitwar

HRATCH BABIKIAN

Red Sea Urchin, 2002
2.5 x 2.5 x 2.5 cm
14-karat gold, sterling silver,
amethyst cabochon;
cast, fabricated
Photo by artist

JUDE CLARKE

Two Faced Rings, 2000
1.5 x 2 x 2.4 cm (each)
Sterling silver, 18-karat gold,
stones; overlaid, fabricated
Photo by Hap Sakwa

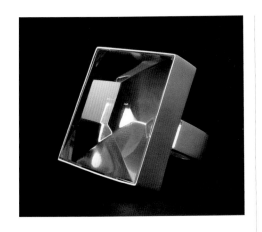

ANNEKE van BOMMEL

Diamond Ring Series, Ring #3, 2003

4 x 4 x 4 cm

Acrylic, sterling silver;

hand carved, cast, fabricated

Photo by artist

BENITA EDWARDS

Peak, the Ring of Luck!, 2002

2.9 x 2 x 1 cm

18-karat rose gold, 18-karat yellow gold,

9-karat white gold, pear shaped sapphires,

diamonds; wax cast

Photo by artist

SANDRA GILES

Communion Table Ring, 2002

3.8 x 3.8 x 3.8 cm

Sterling silver, fine silver, citrine, garnet;

roller printed, hollow constructed

Photo by Charles Lewton-Brain

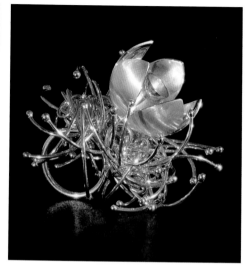

MEI SEE LIANG-JACKSON

Heirloom Series: Receptaculum, 2003

5 x 6 x 4.5 cm

Sterling silver, 18-karat gold;

fabricated

Photo by artist

MARIA PACE PELLEGRINI

Pupa, 2003

4 x 2.8 x 2.4 cm

18-karat gold, Tahitian

pearls; constructed

Photo by Federico Cavicchioli

INGJERD HANEVOLD

Remembering, 2002

11 x 9.5 cm

Bronze, lotus

Photo by artist

HOLLY HAMILTON and ROBIN MARTIN-CUST

Untitled, 2000

1.9 x 1.9 x 1.3 cm (each)

Found pitted steel, 18-karat

yellow gold; fabricated

Photo by Robert Diamante

RAINER HERRMANN

Gewichtung, 2002

3.3 x 4 x 2.1 cm

18-karat gold, rutilated quartz

Photo by Rainer Schäle

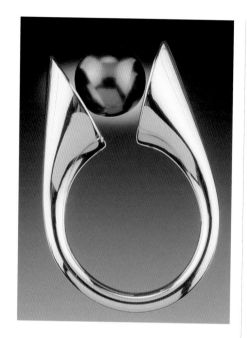

LEE CARPER

Vortex Ring, 2002

2.8 x 1.9 x .8 cm

14-karat yellow gold, 24-karat
gold, Tahitian black pearl;
hollow formed, forged, raised,
shell formed, fabricated

Photo by Jerry Anthony

GINA PANKOWSKI

Pearl Orbit #2, 2001

5.7 x 3.2 x 3.2 cm

18-karat gold, 14-karat gold, diamonds,
pink pearl doublet; fabricated

Photo by Douglas Yaple

Fusion dictated the design and fabrication of this ring. Silver and 18-karat gold were heated to flow point, producing a reticulated shank dotted with gold pallions—dense flower petals. Texturing the surface of the bezel and petals captures a halo around the chatoyant pink quartz.

Nadine Kariya

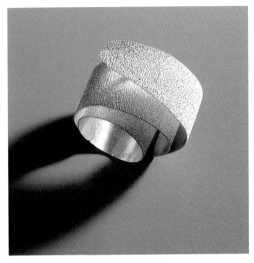

NADINE KARIYA

Blooming Rose Quartz Ring, 2002

3 x 2.5 x 2.6 cm

Sterling silver, fine silver, 18-karat gold, rose quartz cabochon, diamond; fused, formed, fabricated

Photo by Douglas Yaple

ANNAMARIA ZANELLA

Untitled, 1998

3 x 2 cm

Gold

Photo by Lorenzo Trento

JANIS KERMAN

Ring, 2002

3.2 x 1.9 cm

18-karat gold, aquamarine

Photo by Larry Turner

JACLYN DAVIDSON

Zebra Ring, 1996

2.5 x 1.3 x .6 cm

18-karat gold, enamel; cast, filed,

chased, engraved

Photo by Ralph Gabriner

TRAVIS G. T. CONNORS

Sapphire and Garnet Ring, 2003

2.4 x .9 x .4 cm

18-karat gold, 19-karat gold, 19-karat

white gold, fancy orange square sapphires,

tsavorite garnets; constructed, bezel set

Photo by artist

PAM RITCHIE

Mother of Exiles Ring, from the
Cancelled Icons series, 2003
2.5 x 2.2 x 3.6 cm
18-karat gold, sterling silver, gold
leaf, postage stamp; fabricated
Photo by George Georgakakos

KRISTEN L. HOLTVEDT

Expanding Energy, 2003
3.2 x 3.2 x 3.2 cm
14-karat gold, sterling silver;
chased, repoussé
Photos by Tim Lazure

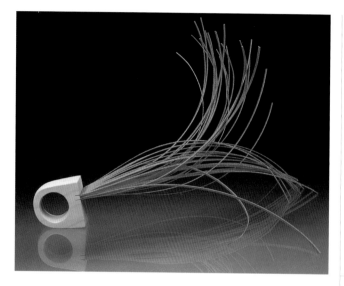

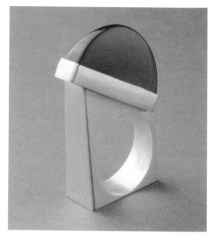

CAROL SAKIHARA

Celebration, 2002

16.5 x 10.2 x 1.9 cm

Wood, red vellum paper; carved

Photo by artist

IWONA DUSZEK

Silence and Light, 1996

3.8 x 2.5 x .9 cm

Silver, copper, agate;

fabricated

Photo by Roman Duszek

＠ **The process of
simplifying elements,
objects, and ideas—
and simplicity itself—
is one of the most
important and
indispensable
parts of my work.**

Iwona Duszek

SABINE KLARNER

Winter Ring, 2002

4 x 4 x 3 cm

Gold, silver, precious stones, fur

Photo by Katrin Gauditz

ROBERT DANCIK

Disc Ring, 2003

9.2 x 9.2 x .6 cm

PVC pipe, sterling silver, fine silver
leaf, carnelian; carved, fabricated

Photo by Ralph Gabriner

MYOUNG SUN LEE

Find Out! (2, 3, 4), 2002

2.2 x 2.2 x .5 cm (each)

Silver, ebony, gold, copper, rose tree

Photos by Myung-Wook Huh (Studio Munch)

MYOUNG SUN LEE

Find Out! (5), 2002

2.2 x 2.2 x .5 cm

Copper, wood

RAMON PUIG CUYÀS

Cap de Berberia, 2002

3 x 2.5 x 1.2 cm

Silver, glass, paper

Photo by artist

CAZ GUINEY

Organic Rings, 1998

2 x 2.2 x 2.2 cm (each)

Red Hill grass, sand, pumice,
dirt; hand built, carved

Photos by Andrew Barcham

MARGOT DOUGLAS

Reef Cocktail Series, 2001

5 x 4.5 x 4 cm (largest)

Sterling silver, shell, beach
glass, pebbles, coral, enamel

Photo by Grant Hancock

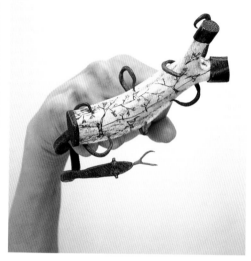

THOMAS HILL

Paradise Knuckleduster, 2003

22.9 x 16.5 x 5 cm (on stand)

Brass, rib bone, American walnut, patina;

forged, painted, engraved, stained

Photos by Jeffrey Goldsmith

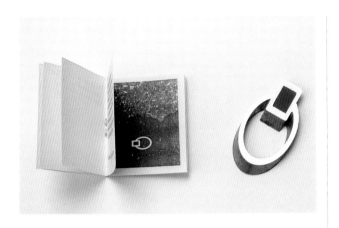

GISBERT STACH

Jewelry for Hot Days, 1996

4.8 x 2.5 x .4 cm

Brass, synthetic resin,

instruction pamphlet; soldered

Photo by artist

KIFF SLEMMONS

One of Us Has to Go: Dueling Squirts, 2002

11.4 x 17.1 x 2.5 cm (box)

Cigar box, sterling silver, satin, plastic;

painted, pierced, fabricated

Photo by Rod Slemmons

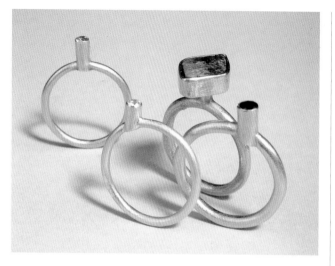

TAMAR KERN

Stackables, 2003

3.8 x 1.9 x .3 cm

18-karat gold, diamonds,

opal, sapphire

Photo by Mark Johnston

NORMAN WEBER

Untitled, 1993

5.8 x 4.1 x 3.4 cm

8-karat gold; soldered

Photo by artist

GERD ROTHMANN

Family Ring, 1992

Gold

2.2 x 2.2 cm

Photo by Wilfried Petzi

GIANCARLO MONTEBELLO

Moghul, 2000

2.8 x 2.3 x .9 cm

18-karat yellow gold, 18-karat white gold

Photo by Ruggero Boschetti

CATHY CHOTARD

Untitled, 1998

1.6 x 2 cm (each)

Silver

Photo by artist

RANDY LONG

Halo and Heaven Wedding Ring Sets, 1995

2.2 x 2.2 x .3 cm (each, top);

2.5 x 2.5 x .6 cm (each, bottom)

18-karat gold, sterling silver, niello;

wax carved, cast

Photo by artist

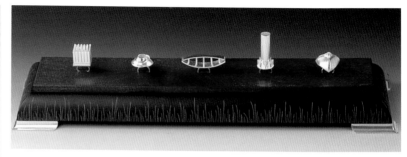

ANNE T. HALLAM

Family Portrait, 2002

11.4 x 61 x 15.2 cm (with base)

Sterling silver, 18-karat bimetal,

18-karat gold, mahogany; fabricated

Photo by artist

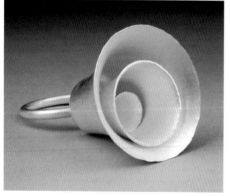

YOON JEONG KIM

Untitled, 1998–2002

Various dimensions

5.5 x 2.2 x 2.5 cm (detail)

Sterling silver, 18-karat gold;

fabricated, hammered

Courtesy of Andora Gallery,

Carefree, Arizona

Photos by Myung-Wook Huh

(Studio Munch)

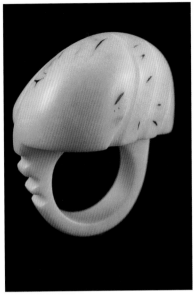

KIFF SLEMMONS

Self-Storage, 1997

3.8 x 13.3 x 3.8 cm (box)

Silver, brass, mica,

photographs; fabricated

Photo by Rod Slemmons

DAVID LaPLANTZ

Mushroom Finger Top, 2002

4.8 x 4.4 x 2.7 cm

Tagua nut; constructed,

fabricated

Photo by artist

JAY SONG

Lantern, 2003

11.4 x 5 x 5 cm

Sterling silver, gold foil; fabricated

Photo by Taweesak Molsawat

KRISTINE BOLHUIS

Ring for the Little Finger, 2001

2.5 x 3.8 x 1.3 cm

Sterling silver, 18-karat gold;

fold formed, hammered

Photo by Dean Powell

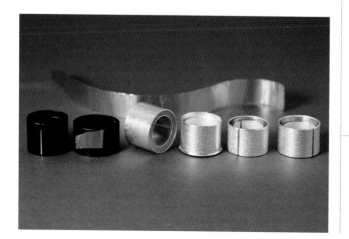

MARGRIT LINDER-HINTERMEISTER

Rings for a Love Letter, 1997–2000

1.8 cm high (each)

Fine gold sheet, silver, blackened iron

Courtesy of Galerie V & V, Vienna, Austria

Photo by artist

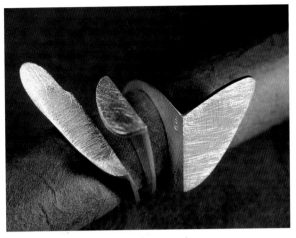

ELIANA R. ARENAS

Rich Simplicity I & II, 2003

5 x 5 x 5 cm (each)

Silver, cubic zirconias;

hollow constructed

Photo by Rachelle Thiewes

NOELLA EUNJU OH

Split Wings, 2003

Various dimensions

Sterling silver

Photo by Amanda McKittrick

HELFRIED KODRÉ

The Golden Branch, 1998

3.5 x 3.5 x 1.2 cm

Gold; soldered

Photo by artist

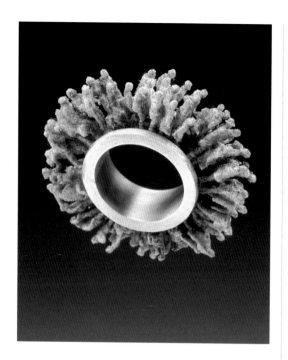

K. DANA KAGRISE

Exodus—09·11·01, 2001

4.4 x 1.3 cm

Sterling silver, pumice, powder
enamel, plastic N-scale model
train figures; fabricated

Photos by Jeff Sabo

Exodus was made in response to the tragic events of September 11, 2001. I was most affected by the photographs of people fleeing the city, many by way of the Brooklyn Bridge. Included in the mass of people I have placed a photographer facing the opposite way to represent the risks that many people took to document the tragedy as it unfolded.

K. Dana Kagrise

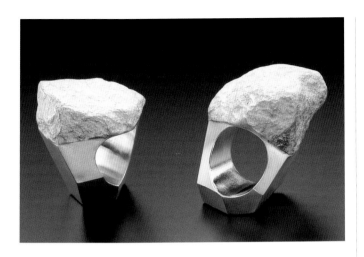

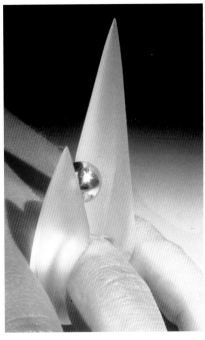

CHEN YuCHUN

Fancying Big Stones, 2002

3 x 3.5 x 2.5 cm

Sterling silver; cast,

hollow constructed

Photo by Federico Cavicchioli

⊕ The world around me is the mother of my emotions. My jewelry works are the children of my time. In this little imaginary world of mine, lines, symbols, colors, and dimensions come together. They interact and create a dialogue of their own, mingling between reality and fantasy. This is a private conversation. The stories are left to be seen in the viewer's eyes.

Chen YuChun

HUAN NGUYEN

Spike, 2003

6.9 x 3.2 x 1.3 cm

Acrylic, aluminum bearing;

hand carved, tension set

Photo by Dean Spencer

CASTELLO HANSEN

Untitled, 2003

5.3 x 3.4 x 3.4 cm

Cibatool®, reconstructed coral,

paint, 18-karat gold

Photo by artist

JASON PENN

Montana Wedding, 2002

2.9 x 2.9 x .7 cm (left); 2.7 x 2.7 x .7 cm (right)

Solid Montana agate, 18-karat gold tube, Arizona

anthill garnet; carved, drilled, frosted, rivet set

Photo by Azad

ANDREA WAGNER

Untitled, 1997

6.5 x 4.5 x 3.5 cm

Silver, garnets, epoxide resin;

cast, set, faceted

Photo by Dominik Schunk

SHEENA THOMAS

High Rise, 1991

5 x 2.2 x 2.2 cm

Sterling silver, amethyst beach

pebble; formed, constructed, set

Photo by Peter Krumhardt

YUKO YAGISAWA

Spirit Ring Series #1:

Cause of My Destiny, 2003

5 x 5 x 2.5 cm

Sterling silver, found objects;

fabricated

Photo by artist

JI-HA PARK

The Rose of Infidelity, 2002

9 x 7 x 1 cm

Acrylic, silver

Photo by Myung-Wook Huh (Studio Munch)

SEO YOON CHOI

Desire, 1999

106 x 16 x 19 cm

Sterling silver, stainless steel, feathers

Photo by Myung-Wook Huh (Studio Munch)

HYE-YOUNG SUH

Coral Ring Series 2, 2003

5 x 2.5 x 1.3 cm (each)

Copper, enamel; electroformed

Photo by artist

EUN-MEE CHUNG

Snow Flower I, 2003

5 x 5 x 8.2 cm

18-karat gold, sterling silver,
diamond, cotton maché

Photo by Myung-Wook Huh
(Studio Munch)

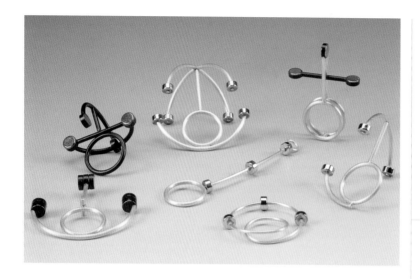

ERICA DUFFY

Magnet Rings, 2002

Various dimensions

3.8 x 3.8 x 3.8 cm (detail)

Sterling silver, brass, magnets;

fabricated

Photos by Jeff Sabo

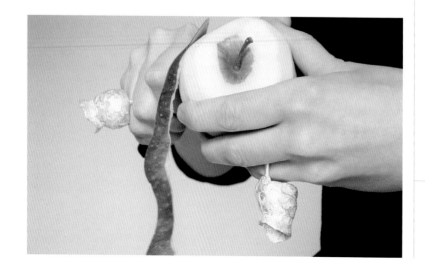

MELANIE SEILER

Pair of Rings, 2003

5 x 2.8 x 2.5 cm (each)

Silver; wax modeled, cast

Photo by Samuel Durling

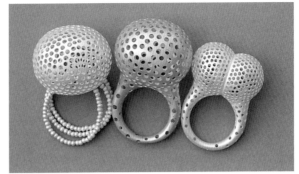

MASCHA MOJE

3 Rings, 2000
Various dimensions
3 x 2 x 1.5 cm (detail)
Silver; hollow constructed,
raised, soldered, drilled
Photos by artist

FRIEDRICH MÜLLER

Quadratur Deskreises
(Quadrature of the Circle), 2001
2.9 x 1.7 x .6 cm
Hard plastic (Ertacetal® Pom);
turned, filed, polished
Photo by Michel Jaussi

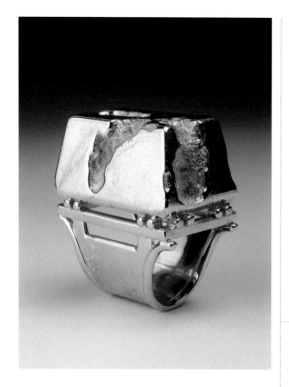

CHRISTINA T. MILLER

A Trophy Ring, 2003

3.2 x 1.9 x 3.2 cm

Sterling silver, 18-karat gold

plate; cast, fabricated

Photo by artist

DORIS MANINGER

Three Times, 2002

4 x .2 cm

Eighteenth-century astrolabe segment,

22-karat gold coin; milled, cut, riveted

Photo by Federico Cavicchioli

● I am an observer. My work is usually concept driven. The objective of the *Introspective Ring* design is to re-identify the functions of jewelry. What is the meaning of wearing a piece of jewelry when glamour will be hidden as soon as you put it on? This ring keeps its value inside and provides an extraordinary sensation for the wearer. I question the way we view a piece of jewelry, but metaphorically I question the way we present ourselves and the way we perceive others.

Nick Dong

NICK DONG

Introspective Ring, 2003

2.3 x 2.3 x .7 cm

18-karat yellow gold,

24-karat yellow gold, garnets;

fabricated, bezel set

Photo by Hap Sakwa

HELFRIED KODRÉ

Sambruson, 2000

3 x 2.2 x 2.2 cm

Gold, white gold, citrine;

soldered

Photo by artist

JOËL DEGEN

5 Rings, 2003

Various dimensions

18-karat yellow gold, titanium,

diamond baguettes, diamond

brilliants; riveted

Photo by artist

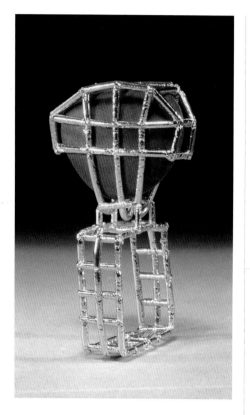

CHARLES LEWTON-BRAIN

Cage Ring: Stone B385, 2002

5 x 2.5 x 3.5 cm

Stainless steel wire, copper,

24-karat gold, Nova Scotia beach

stone; fusion welded, electroformed

Photo by artist

GIOVANNI CORVAJA

Untitled, 1996
2.3 x 2.3 x 2.3 cm (left);
2.5 x 4.2 x 3 cm (right)
22-karat gold, niello, platinum,
diamond; granulated
Photo by artist

C. JAMES MEYER

Ring, 1996
2.2 x 2.5 x 3.8 cm
18-karat green gold, opal,
beach glass; fabricated
Photo by Taylor Dabney

KYUNG-HEE KIM

Episode of Ring II: Floating in Silence, 2003
Various dimensions
Sterling silver, gold leaf; kum-boo
Photo by Myung-Wook Huh (Studio Munch)

TOMOMI ARATA

Treasures from Under the Sea, 2003

4.9 x 2.7 x 1.4 cm

Silver, enamel, sand, pearl;

hand cast

Photo by Minoru Hashimoto

CHIH-WEN CHIU

Untitled, 2003

5.7 x 3.2 x 2.5 cm

Copper, synthetic ruby;

hammered, textured, set

Photos by Dan Neuberger

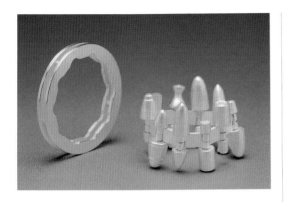

DANIEL HUYNH

Ring for a Broken Finger I, 2003

7.6 x 5 x 5 cm

Sterling silver, white Delrin®;

fabricated, chased

Photo by artist

WOOK KOH

A Limit, 2003

1.8 x 2.5 cm

Sterling silver;

hinged, cast, riveted

Photos by Myung-Wook Huh

(Studio Munch)

413

INDEX

CRISTINA FILIPE ...il est tout plat, et il a une emeraude, la plus belle que j'aie jamais vue, 1997
60 x 40 x 1 cm; flowers, field. Photo by artist